Clarence A. (Clarence Augustus) Walworth

Reminiscences of Edgar P. Wadhams: First Bishop of Ogdensburg

Clarence A. (Clarence Augustus) Walworth
Reminiscences of Edgar P. Wadhams: First Bishop of Ogdensburg
ISBN/EAN: 9783743462847
Manufactured in Europe, USA, Canada, Australia, Japa
Cover: Foto ©ninafisch / pixelio.de

Manufactured and distributed by brebook publishing software (www.brebook.com)

Clarence A. (Clarence Augustus) Walworth

Reminiscences of Edgar P. Wadhams: First Bishop of Ogdensburg

RIGHT REV. E. P. WADHAMS, D.D.,
First Bishop of Ogdensburg, N. Y.

REMINISCENCES

OF

EDGAR P. WADHAMS,

First Bishop of Ogdensburg.

Rev. C. A. WALWORTH,

Author of "The Gentle Skeptic," "Andiatorocte, and Other Poems," etc.

WITH A PREFACE

By Right Rev. H. GABRIELS, D.D.,
Bishop of Ogdensburg.

SECOND EDITION.

New York, Cincinnati, Chicago:

BENZIGER BROTHERS,

Printers to the Holy Apostolic See.

PREFACE.

THE following pages have already been appreciated by the readers of the *Catholic World* as a tribute of faith and of friendship.

A tribute of faith. Both the subject and the author of the Reminiscences were actors in that great tractarian movement which brought thousands out of the labyrinth of Protestantism into the one Christian fold, and which, moreover, infused into non-Catholic denominations that new religious leaven by which they are lifted up every day nearer and nearer to the truth. To few was it known how lively this movement had been on this side of the ocean, and how many Americans, Episcopalians principally, had been either led by it into the Catholic Church, or stimulated to adopt many of her doctrines and rites. Father Walworth gives us a vivid description of those memorable years, and it is not without a desire for more that we peruse the documents which it was his good luck to discover among the papers of the first bishop of Ogdensburg. No Catholic will read his reminiscences without feeling happier with him and his illustrious brother-convert for the possession of the one true religion and without praying that those friends of theirs, who are still wavering at the entrance, may like them receive the kiss of welcome from the Master of the fold.

The book is a tribute of friendship. United less by the tie of kindred than by that of affection and of common aspirations, Bishop Wadhams and Father Walworth, like Basil and Gregory, attended the same schools; like Newman and Froude, they communed together on the light that was leading them on, until finally the one helped the other to take the decisive step that made them denizens of the City of God. No wonder that their souls remained knit and that Virgil was half of the soul of his Horace. It was fitting that when one was called to his reward, the other should put in writing some of the words and deeds by which the departed had deserved remembrance, either as the neophyte who had with him piously accepted the Divine message, or as the priest and prelate who had taught and ruled for the salvation of many, or as a partisan of sacred truth who knew how to mingle the largest kindness with controversy, or in fine as the citizen and friend who, by his patriotism and his genial disposition, had endeared himself to all:

" Qui didicit patriæ quid debeat, et quid amicis,
Quo sit amore parens, quo frater amandus, et hospes;
Quod sit conscripti, quod judicis officium; quæ
Partes in bellum missi ducis."

The proceeds of the sale of this book will be applied to missionary labor in behalf of the Catholic Iroquois of this diocese.

✠ H. GABRIELS.

OGDENSBURG, Feast of St. Pius V., 1893.

Contents.

	PAGE
PREFACE,	3
INTRODUCTORY,	9

CHAPTER I.

Wadhams at the Episcopalian Seminary.—His Associates There.—Some Off-hand Recollections, . . . 15

CHAPTER II.

Correspondence between Wadhams and Old Associates at the Seminary.—Efforts to Establish Monastic Life. 1841–1844, ... 35

CHAPTER III.

A Storm at Oxford Echoed at the Chelsea Seminary.—Sindbad's Whale Flops.—The Cloister Goes Under.—Friends Cross Over to Rome. 1845, . . . 62

CHAPTER IV.

Wadhams and the Encircling Gloom.—"Lead Thou Me On."—Nostrums Against Romanism.—He Enters the Fold. 1845-1846, ... 92

CHAPTER V.

Wadhams' Life at the Sulpician Seminary, Baltimore. 1846–1850, ... 123

CHAPTER VI.

PAGE

Wadhams' Priesthood at St. Mary's Church and at the Cathedral, Albany.—The War of the Rebellion.—His Trip to Europe and the Holy Land. 1850-1872, . 138

CHAPTER VII.

Wadhams Becomes Bishop of Ogdensburg.—His Life and Labors in the New Diocese.—His Sufferings and Sudden Cure.—Trials.—His Last Illness and Death. 1872-1891, ... 159

APPENDIX.

The Wadhams Family in England and America, . . 193

Introductory.

THE object of the author is not to write a biography of Bishop Wadhams or any systematic sketch of his life. This I leave to other hands. I simply wish to record certain familiar memories I retain of that early and dear friend which might otherwise be lost; memories of his early home and surroundings in the Adirondacks; memories of those seminary days when with myself and others he was moving forward, in an Anglican atmosphere of mingled beliefs, romances, and illusions, toward the clear light and settled doctrine of the Catholic Church; memories of his priestly life, during a part of which I was his close companion, and memories also of a frequent and sweet intercourse which continued throughout his career in the episcopate, and ended only with his death. These reminiscences may be welcomed as valuable by some of my readers, partly because of the marked individuality of the man, and partly because of his early connection with a religious movement memorable in the history of our American Church, but better known to Catholics generally in its effects than in its causes or progressive course. One born to the faith looks upon the accession of converts into the Church as a man watches an incoming tide. He sees the waves fall tired on the shore, but cannot see what draws them or what drives them, or understand that panting but unsatisfied life out of which they leap. Perhaps the following pages may open to some of my readers a better knowledge of the external events and a clearer view of the interior springs of action by which a convert's course is urged and guided.

Before, however, I take up my personal recollections of my friend, it is proper to give some account of his birth, boyhood, and college life, which I am obliged to gather from the recollections of others.

Edgar P. Wadhams was born May 21st, 1817, in the town of Lewis, Essex County, New York. He was the sixth and youngest child of General Luman Wadhams and his wife Lucy. His father, Luman, a native of Goshen, Connecticut, settled early in life at Charlotte, Vermont, and afterward moved to Lewis, in Essex County, New York. He finally fixed his residence in the adjoining town of Westport, giving name to the village of Wadhams Mills, where he died April 19th, 1832, in the fiftieth year of his age. He was an officer at the battle of Plattsburgh, and rose to the rank of general in the militia service. His wife, Lucy Prindle (*née* Bostwick), the mother of Edgar, was a woman of great piety as well as remarkable for sagacity, and a wondrous wisdom born of both these qualities. To her thoughtful care, pious moral training, and the example she gave by her conscientious discharge of every duty, is no doubt due in great part that life of manly principle and nobility of soul which always characterized the subject of these reminiscences. I knew her well, resided in the same house with her for several months, conversing with her daily, and have never lost the impression made upon me by a certain simple but marvellous tact she possessed which amounted to true wisdom. She survived her husband, General Wadhams, many years, living to see her son a priest, and died at the advanced age of eighty-four. Her body, as well as that of her husband, lies buried at Wadhams Mills.

We are not able to give much detail in regard to Edgar's childhood. There is, perhaps, no necessity for it. Let it suffice to say that there is testimony to the fact that from his earliest years Edgar was looked upon as a boy of great promise. He was sent to an academy at Shoreham, Vermont, where he prepared for college. He entered Middlebury College in 1834, enrolling himself in the freshman class of that year. Some account of his course at this college is important, not only to show what manner of man he was at that time, but because it was there that, although reared a Presbyterian, he became attracted toward Anglicanism, which he mistook for something Catholic, and was led to unite himself to the Protestant Episcopal Church.

We are indebted to the Rev. J. Avery Shepherd, now an Episcopalian clergyman living in California, for nearly all we know of Wadhams' college career. There was a family connection between the two. Wadhams' sister, Mrs. Weeks, was the wife of Shepherd's uncle. It was at her house, six miles distant from Middlebury, that the two friends first met when about to enter that college. They were classmates, and roomed together during the ensuing four years. Shepherd was a Baptist, but up to this time Wadhams, although born of Presbyterian parents, had never enrolled himself as a professed member of any Christian denomination. It was at Middlebury that Wadhams, to use his friend's expression, "became serious." He was observed to take off his hat when passing the Episcopal church. He soon obtained permission from the college authorities to attend service there. We are told also that on rising in the morning, which he did at four o'clock, he was accustomed to read aloud for one hour from Chapman's *Sermons on Episcopacy*. His friend when awaking would listen to this, although pretending to sleep. He had urged Wadhams to become a Baptist, but either Chapman's sermons or Wadhams himself proved more persuasive, and after about three months both were churchmen, and both active church members. In fact, these two students ran the whole thing at Middlebury. There being no settled minister, they officiated alternately, Wadhams playing the organ when the other read the service, and *vice versa*.

Wadhams graduated with honors from Middlebury College in 1838. From this same college he received the degree of LL.D. a short time previous to his death.

Reminiscences of Edgar P. Wadhams,

First Bishop of Ogdensburg.

Chapter 1.

Wadhams at the Episcopalian Seminary.—His Associates There.—Some Off-hand Recollections at the Outset, Intended to Characterize the Man.

MY first acquaintance with Bishop Wadhams began with the beginning of autumn in 1842. At that time I entered the General Theological Seminary of the Protestant Episcopal Church in New York City, situated on Twentieth Street at the corner of Ninth Avenue. Edgar P. Wadhams, if I remember right, began at that time his third and last year at that seminary. I felt much interested in him, partly as being a kinsman in no very remote degree, but still more by a certain frankness, heartiness, and moral nobility of character, which made him very attractive to all who knew him. Many of those who were in the seminary at that time have since made their mark in life, but need not be especially mentioned here. The most remarkable inmate of the institution at that time, and a most familiar friend of Wadhams, was Arthur Carey, a graduate of 1842, but still retaining his room at the seminary as being too young to receive orders. The moral beauty of Carey's character was of the highest type, and his intellectual superiority was also something wonderful. His influence upon Wadhams was very great, as indeed it was upon many more of us, while Carey himself was a devoted disciple of John Henry Newman, then a resident at Oxford, and afterwards a priest and cardinal of the Catholic Church. When, about a year after his graduation, Carey's name was put on the list of candidates for admission to the ministry, a protest against his ordination was made to Bishop Onderdonk by Dr. Anthon, of St. Mark's Church, and by Dr. Smith, of St. Peter's Church in Twentieth Street. He was charged with "Romanizing" tendencies. A committee of eight clergymen was appointed by the bishop to try him. On the committee were Drs. Smith and Anthon, his accusers, and Dr. Seabury, also a pastor in the city. Dr. Seabury published all the proceedings of the trial in the New York *Churchman*, of which he was then editor. Carey was closely questioned, but, young as he was, the acuteness of his mind and the accuracy of his learning were so far in advance of his accusers that they were subjected to constant confusion, and unable to push their inquiries as far as they would for fear of betraying their ignorance. This gave much amusement to Dr. Seabury, who was friendly to Carey, and afterwards to many readers of the *Churchman*. Bishop Onderdonk and the majority of the examining committee acquitted Carey of unsoundness in his doctrine, and soon after he presented himself to receive ordination. The ceremony took place at St. Stephen's Church, New York. This ceremony was interrupted in a manner so solemn and so startling that no one there present can ever forget it. The bishop, before the laying on of hands, solemnly addressed the congregation and demanded: "If there be any one here present who has aught to say why any of these candidates should not receive," etc.—"let him come forth in the name of God." To the astonishment of all, Dr. Smith, of St. Peter's, arose in the middle of the church and protested against the ordination of Arthur Carey. The protest was couched in the most solemn language, beginning, if I remember right: "In the name of the Father, and of the Son, and of the Holy Ghost. Amen," etc.

When Dr. Smith sat down, the Rev. Dr. Anthon arose and made a like protest with the same solemn formality. The charges of both were the same, namely, that Arthur Carey was unfaithful to the doctrine of his own church and imbued with the errors of Rome. The sensation that followed was something fearful, though the silence was profound. My father, who sat beside me, trembled from head to foot, and turned to me with a look of awe and wonder which I can never forget. "The bishop will ordain him all the same," said I. When Carey's accusers had finished their protest, Bishop Onderdonk arose from his seat and addressed the congregation. His attitude was majestic. He looked indignant and determined. He informed the congregation that the charges against Arthur Carey were not then brought forward for the first time; that he had already given him a trial upon the same complaints; that the same accusers had been appointed among his judges then; and that Carey had been acquitted at that trial as perfectly sound in the faith. The bishop praised him also as eminently fitted for orders both by his great talents and by the moral beauty of his character. "Therefore," he said, "I shall now proceed to ordain Mr. Carey with the other candidates, in spite of the scandalous interruption of these reverend protesters." All present then breathed again with a deep feeling of relief, and the ceremonies went on to the end.

As memory serves me, among those ordained to a deaconship at that time was Edgar P. Wadhams. He loved Carey and sympathized with him fully. Carey died at the close of the following winter, on his way to Cuba, and was buried in the ocean. Wadhams and I were in company when the intelligence of his death came, and we mourned for him as men mourn for a brother.

RIGHT REV. HENRY GABRIELS, D.D.,
Present Bishop of Ogdensburg, N. Y.

Besides myself, several of Wadhams' companions at this Episcopal Seminary have since become Catholics. The first was Edward Putnam, who left the seminary for that purpose in 1844. He became a priest and officiated for a while at St. Mary's Church, Albany, in 1848 and 1849, a short time before Father Wadhams' ministrations in the same parish.

An intimate friend and companion at the seminary both of Wadhams and Carey was James A. McMaster, a very peculiar and notable character, both when at that institution and during many long years afterwards as editor of a very influential and popular Catholic periodical, the *Freeman's Journal*. McMaster should, in the natural course of things, have been ordained at the same time with Carey and Wadhams. He was, however, too troublesome a responsibility for Bishop Onderdonk to carry. Not only were his tendencies toward Rome very decided, but he loved to make that fact stand out. He was always delighted when his strong enunciations of belief or opinion spread alarm in the Protestant camp. It became necessary to sacrifice McMaster in order to carry Carey and others through.

Whicher, another companion of Wadhams at the seminary, was ordained a year later, and became pastor of an Episcopal church at Clayville, Oneida County, N. Y. About ten years later he became a Catholic. The late Monsignor Preston, vicar-general and chancellor of the

Archdiocese of New York, a distinguished convert of this period, entered the seminary after Wadhams' departure, but in time to make acquaintance there with some students of the same circle and stamp. He moved into my room when I left it, saying, with what he intended for a great compliment, "I am happy to enter into quarters *so decidedly Catholic.*" The full pith of this remark can scarcely be understood by those whose experience has never made them familiar with the Oxford movement, and who cannot remember, as Bishop Wadhams could, how rife this General Seminary was at that time with the air of Puseyism, which had a marked phraseology of its own, generally earnest enough, but having also its humorous side.

Father William Everett, for so many years pastor of the Church of the Nativity in New York City, was a classmate and friend of Wadhams at the seminary, and one of the leading spirits there among that class of students who aimed at being catholic without any intention at the time of becoming Catholics. He entered the church in 1851.

On receiving deacon's orders in the Episcopal Church, Wadhams was assigned to duty in Essex County, N. Y., the whole county, if we remember right, being included in his jurisdiction, his principal station being at Ticonderoga, with occasional services at Wadhams Mills and Port Henry. I maintained a correspondence with him during the remainder of my own stay at the seminary, and in the autumn of 1844, or early in 1845, I joined him in Essex County. My eyesight had so far failed me that for the time being I could not prosecute my studies. I longed for his society, and at the same time we had initiated a plan, very sincere but romantic enough to be sure, for introducing something like the monastic life into the North Woods. Another student of the seminary was also in the scheme, who proposed to join us later in the year when he should have graduated. I carried with me a full copy of the Breviary, in four volumes; for we anticipated a time to come when we should grow into a full choir of monks and chant the office. We spent much of our time that winter at Ticonderoga village. Later, however, we established ourselves more permanently at Wadhams Mills, lodging with his mother, who lived alone in the old house. We occupied two bedrooms and another large room, which we used as a carpenter-shop, for we had learned that monks must labor with their hands when not occupied with prayer or study. We boarded ourselves, that is, we did our own cooking. I officiated as cook, occasionally helped by my friend. We did pretty well at first, aided by the instructions and supervision of the old lady, although she occasionally laughed at us, as when our fingers stuck in the dough, or when she found the bread all burned to a crisp for want of watching.

Wadhams' favorite idea was to educate boys of the neighborhood, training them specially to a religious life, which should serve finally to stock our convent with good monks. A handful of boys who gathered with other children on Sundays in the school-house for catechism seemed to afford a nucleus which might afterwards develop into a novitiate.

We actually laid the foundations and built up the sides of a convent building. It was nothing, indeed, but a log-house and never received a roof, for the winter was intensely cold and the ensuing spring opened with events which sent me into the Catholic Church and to Europe, leaving nothing of the convent but roofless logs and a community of one. But I mistake; Wadhams had a Canadian pony which, in honor of pious services to be thereafter rendered, we named *Béni*, and a cow which for similar reasons we named *Bonté*.

Our log-house cloister was built on a lovely spot under the shelter of a hill which bounded a farm inherited by Wadhams from his father. The farm contained a fine stretch of woodland on the south, while the greater part from east to west was open and cultivated field, the half of which, high and terraced, looked down upon a lower meadow-land which extended on a perfect level to a fine stream bordering the farm on the east. Beyond the brook and along its edge ran the road from Wadhams Mills to Lewis.

There was much debate before we fixed on the site of our convent. A fine barn stood already built on the natural terrace near the south side, while under the terrace at the north end was a magnificent spring of the purest water. Where should the convent be, near the barn or near the spring? Every present convenience lay on the side of the barn, and the horse and cow were actual possessions. But our hopes looked brightly into the future. What would a great community of hooded cenobites do without a holy well near by? So we laid the foundations of the future pile on the edge of the terrace just above the spring. We did not consult either *Béni* or *Bonté*.

In the mean while Wadhams and myself endeavored to practise, in such ways as actual circumstances would permit, a religious life, the truest type of which we even then believed to be found in the Catholic Church, though our knowledge of it was very imperfect. We commenced Lent with a determination to fast every day on one meal alone and that not before three o'clock, with no meat, not even on Sundays. As we worked hard in our carpenter-shop besides other physical exercises, this privation soon began to tell upon us. I took the cooking upon myself, he assisting in washing the dishes. My principal talent lay in cooking *mush*. This agreed with me and I throve on it very well, but Wadhams, who was large, strong, and full-blooded, and to whom fasting was always something very severe, began after a time to look pale and wild. "Look here," said he one day—"look here, Walworth! This mush may agree with a fellow like you, who have no body to speak of; but I can't stand it. I don't want to eat meat, but you must give me something else besides mush." "All right," said I, "you shall have something better to-morrow." So I killed a fat chicken and got Mother Wadhams to show me how to prepare and cook it. When my friend came in for dinner I pointed it out to him triumphantly. "But," said he, "I can't eat meat in Lent!" "Well," said I, "I don't want you to. That is *chicken*." I really believed that chicken was allowed among Catholics, and succeeded in convincing him. We found Lent much easier after that.

It was not easy for Wadhams to make the necessary rounds through Essex County in the winter-time. When starting from Wadhams Mills he could always command a horse and sleigh, but when setting out from other points he was often obliged to trudge through the deep snow for many miles on foot, to the great admiration even of the hardy inhabitants of the North Woods, who wondered at his sturdy strength as well as at his zeal. His fondness for children was remarkable. He would often rein in his horse or stop in his walks to question some strange child on the road. "Where do you live? What is your name?" he would ask; and always "Have you been baptized?" and "Do you say your prayers?" And if answered favorably, he added, "Good for you; that's the kind of boy to meet!" He took me with him to witness a baptism. It was somewhere in the neighborhood of Port Henry. There was a whole family to be baptized, as I now remember, nine in number, all on their knees ranged in a row along the kitchen floor, which was the biggest room in the house. The zealous deacon did not spare the water. I held the basin, which was nearly empty when he got through, while the children and the floor were wet enough. He had no faith in sprinkling. It may seem that the surroundings of this ceremony were not very solemn, but I never saw people more deeply impressed by a religious rite than these poor, simple cottagers.

The frank, open, guileless simplicity and energy of Edgar Wadhams' character, and a certain moral heroism which was always his, made his influence magnetic whenever any call to duty roused him into action. He then took command, and there were very few who felt like resisting. He had received the impression that a certain gentleman, a familiar friend and parishioner at one of his stations, frequented too often the village inn. There may have been nothing very serious in the matter, but he was a man of high character and influence, and a good church member. Mr. Wadhams felt it his duty to interfere. He announced his determination to me, and asked me to help him in drawing up a pledge to keep away from that inn, which he intended to make him sign. The gentleman was himself a man of great energy and pride of character, a captain of one of the lake boats, and more accustomed to command than to obey. "All right," I said, "go ahead. He won't sign it, but it may do him some good to see it." "He will sign it," was the reply. "I should like to know how he will get out of it." The captain was thunderstruck. "Who told you to bring this to me?" said he. "Did ——?" (naming a common friend). "No matter about that," was the resolute rejoinder. "There it is, and you must sign it." He did sign it. His own strong nature yielded in the presence of a pure and noble spirit the magnetism of which he himself, a true man, could not help but recognize.

The idea of marrying never seems to have occupied Wadhams' mind. From the time of his entering upon the study of divinity the marriage state for him was out of all question. His views in regard to all clerical celibacy are plainly and strongly stated in a correspondence between himself and an old school-fellow, a candidate for orders also, like himself. This correspondence took place in 1843, while Wadhams, then an Episcopalian, had just begun his career of deacon in Essex County. His friend, already uxorious in intention and very garrulous on the subject of girls, took occasion to consult his old classmate. The reply came in a letter from Port

Henry, dated October 18th, 1843. A few extracts will suffice to show Wadhams' deep aversion to the idea of a married clergy. It amounts to an abhorrence:

"My view of a priest is, that he is a man so long as he remains unmarried, and as soon as he is married he is an old granny. . . . I am not a fit person to ask advice upon this subject. My prejudices are wholly and forever against a married clergy. They are generally a fat, lazy, self-indulgent, good-for-nothing, time-serving race. . . . To your second argument, that there is not enough to keep a celibate employed, I know not what to reply."

Of course no reply could be made by a young minister to such an argument as this, without strange thoughts of the value of a church and clergy where so little occasion for clerical work could exist.

The question of clerical celibacy was one much mooted amongst Episcopalians at this time, and particularly by the students at the General Seminary. One party strongly decried the marriage of clergymen as un-Catholic, and professed to see the seminary surrounded by old maids, spreading their snares for unfledged seminarians. On the other hand, the evangelical party with equal vehemence denounced celibacy as popish and a revival of that heretical doctrine, "forbidding to marry," against which St. Paul cautioned the early Christians. A practical joke was played at the seminary upon one of the students, an earnest opponent of celibacy, by pinning against his door a pair of baby stockings, underneath which was written, "A plea against popery!" Such discussions, of course, had contributed to augment Wadhams' aversion to marriage.

During my visit to him in Essex County, and in the spring of that year, we found time to spend a few days in Montreal. To us, whose minds were so strongly inclined to the old church and the old faith, the chief attraction was the desire to see a Catholic city, and the Catholic life and Catholic institutions which abounded there. When we came to the coast of the St. Lawrence, opposite Montreal, the river was breaking up and not yet free from floating ice. There was no way to cross except in batteaux, and though the boatmen assured us the passage was sufficiently safe, it looked highly dangerous; in fact the flood was so high that an American gentleman and lady who, like us, were on their way to Montreal, were afraid to cross, and much time was lost while the boatmen were urging them to get into the batteau. A French gentleman belonging to Montreal was there also, and, wearied by the delay, succeeded in rousing their courage by appealing to their religious pride. "Come, come, my friends!" said he, "don't be alarmed. You are, I am sure, good Protestants, and ought not to be afraid to die. If you do, you'll go straight to heaven without any purgatory. I am nothing but a poor papist and full of sin; and yet you see I am not afraid. *Entrez, monsieur; entrez, madame!*"

We were anxious to hear the boatmen sing. In those days all the world was familiar with the "Canadian Boatman's Song," but not every one had heard Canadians sing it. The men were too much occupied with their labor to be in a humor to sing. We would not have pressed the point; but our French companion, who seemed to be a man of authority and well known to them, insisted upon it, and stood up to enforce his orders. "Yes, messieurs, they shall sing for you. *Chantez! mes frères, chantez! Quoi! Chantez, dis-je!*" They did sing, and we had romance enough to enjoy it, although not a little alarmed by the wild riding of the boat and the blocks of ice that surrounded us. "Great Christopher!" said Wadhams, "this is glorious."

In Montreal we cared little to see anything except its churches, its convents, and its religious services. At the Gray Nuns' we each bought a rosary. We inquired with much interest whether these were blessed, but were informed that this was not done before selling, and that we must apply to a priest to get them blessed for our special use. Of course, not being of the true fold, we were not in a condition to get this done. We did the next best thing to this that we could think of. We dipped them into the holy-water font at Notre Dame. This was done on the sly.

To us, who knew little at that time of the history of Montreal, and of the interest which old traditions attach to so many of its localities, the chief point of attraction was this great parish church of Notre Dame. Its size astonished us, but the religious novelties which we witnessed there were still more wonderful. Conscious of our ignorance, we were afraid of committing some transgression at each step. We felt devout enough to kneel at every altar, but were afraid of exposing ourselves to ridicule by some blunder. A young Frenchman took us to Vespers with him. When the "*pain bénit*" was handed around through the pews our Catholic friend told us to take some and eat it; but utterly ignorant of what it was, we dared not even touch it, though he laughed when he saw us shrink from it and said it wouldn't hurt us.

To Wadhams' musical ear the chanting at this church opened a new world of religious delight. In the sanctuary stood rows of chanters in rich copes. Their singing was followed at times by a burst of music from the organ-loft. A crowd of children lifted up their voices from one of the galleries. This was supplemented by another crowd of children whose echo came in with a new surprise from the opposite gallery. All this may seem very commonplace to those who began life as Catholics, heirs of the faith and "to the manner born," and who live near to cathedrals or large churches. These can have no idea of the effects produced on the minds of men brought up in the barrenness of Protestantism by the infinite variety of thought and worship in the great church Catholic. Perhaps it is to his remembrance of these services at Notre Dame that so many of our New York congregations owe the combination of choir and sanctuary music first introduced at the Albany Cathedral by Bishop Wadhams, when he was its rector.

Shortly after this visit to Montreal, and about the opening of the summer of 1845, I left my friend for New York City in order to enter the Catholic Church. We parted with great regret, but his mind was in no mood to undertake to dissuade me from my purpose. When, however, I urged him to go with me—"Don't hurry me, Walworth," he said; "I am in a position of responsibility and confidence, and when I leave, if leave I must, it shall be done handsomely. You have no charge. You have only to let your bishop know what you are about doing, and then do it."

I have no recollections nor any data to show in what way Wadhams announced and perfected his withdrawal from the Anglican body. He was not a man to neglect any necessary civilities, nor to forget any kindly relations which had existed between him and early associates in religion. That he was cautious, however, as well as frank and generous, appears from the following fact. When asked to send in a formal renunciation of the Episcopal ministry, he did not think proper to do so. Perhaps he thought this might seem to imply a recognition on his part of some validity in the deacon's orders which he had received in that sect. It was far from his mind to acknowledge the Anglican body as a branch—even a dead branch—of the true Catholic Church.

I carried out my own purpose by a letter from me to my diocesan, Bishop De Lancey, of Western New York, asking him to take my name off from his list of candidates for orders. This letter crossed on its way one from him directing me to come to Geneva for ordination. I then went to New York, where I made my profession of faith in the Church of the Holy Redeemer in Third Street, and soon after left, in company with McMaster and Isaac Hecker, for the Redemptorist novitiate at St. Trond, in Belgium. Wadhams became a Catholic the following year. A letter to me, addressed from Baltimore, brought the announcement of this happy event. I cannot find the letter itself, but one characteristic passage in it is pretty well fixed in my memory. I had just before written to him giving some account of our convent life at St. Trond. "It's all right," said he; "I am a Catholic now as well as yourself. But don't talk to me about your convent rules and routine for getting up early, reciting the office, meditating, fasting, discipline, recreations, and mortifications, and all that sort of thing. I have just been scoured through a general confession. You can't beat that."

After our separation in 1845, which took place at the steamboat landing near Ticonderoga, we did not meet again until the winter of 1851, when I was a missionary and he a priest at Albany in the household of Bishop McCloskey, and officiating at St. Mary's, then the cathedral of that diocese. We were afterwards together once more for a year at the new cathedral in Bishop Conroy's time, and continued to live near each other in the same city until his consecration as Bishop of Ogdensburg, and his departure for that see. He was pleased with his appointment and displayed no affectation of humility in regard to it. "You must feel somewhat depressed," I said to him, "in view of all this new responsibility." He replied, "No, I don't. I like it first rate." He asked me to draw a device for his official seal. Looking upon him as an apostle to the cold region of the Adirondacks, and venturing upon a poor joke, I drew an iceberg, with a sled drawn by a reindeer at the foot of it, and above it the north star. The motto which I chose for him, suggested by this star, was "*Iter para tutum*." "Well," said he, "I like the motto and the star, but we don't need any icebergs or reindeer at Ogdensburg." He was much attached to the district embraced in his diocese and to all its interests. "Hang it!" said he once with great animation, "I should like the people of New York to find out that we are something better than a convenient water-shed."

Chapter II.

Correspondence between Wadhams and Old Associates at the Seminary.—Efforts to Establish Monastic Life.

1841–1844.

I HAVE now so far drawn on my personal reminiscences of Bishop Wadhams as to present to the reader a general and, as I trust, a characteristic sketch of the man, such as nature and divine grace conspired to make him. It is, if I have succeeded in my design, a picture which may serve as frontispiece to what follows. I propose now to go over the same general ground again, and by producing letters which have come into my hands, chiefly such letters as he had himself treasured up from his correspondents, to show him in such light as the eyes of friendship saw him, more especially during that momentous transition time which led him and so many other converts, both in England and in the United States, into the bosom of the holy Catholic Church.

One of the earliest of these letters is from James Lloyd Breck, a young friend of Wadhams, in sympathy, like himself, with Newman, Carey, and others. Breck was at Nashotah, in Wisconsin. His letter is dated "October 21st, 1842." The Nashotah mission was a somewhat romantic attempt to found an Episcopal monastery in the Northwest. Breck was the "superior" or "prior." Besides the superior, the *community* at this time consisted of one assured member, the Rev. William Adams, who was at the head of the school department, while Breck labored on the mission as evangelist. The number of scholars in this school is not stated in the letter, but, as the writer assures us, "the foundation of a permanent church school, in all respects adapted to the most Catholic principles," had been laid. A seminary was also embraced in this institution, and thus far had a nest-egg consisting of one seminarian. The size of the institute at this time may be estimated from the dimensions of the building, which measured thirteen feet by seventeen feet. It consisted of one room only, which served as kitchen, study, sleeping apartment, etc., for the whole community. Two vocations for this monastery had not turned out well. A young clergyman, the son of an Episcopal bishop, had felt obliged to absent himself too frequently, for too long periods, from the cloister. Another difficulty was that he had engaged himself to be married. The other applicant had been found too scrupulous. Breck and Adams were only deacons as yet, and the applicant, who was in priest's orders,

BISHOP WADHAMS' BIRTHPLACE, LEWIS, N. Y.

considered it as not canonical or rubrical to have a private communion service for their benefit. The household had, in consequence, soon been reduced to the slender community already stated. In his letter the reverend superior earnestly urges Wadhams to come and join them.

"If," he writes, "dear Wadhams, you conclude to come, remember we receive you on the ground of our first principles, which are: (1) so long as connected with this institution to remain unmarried; (2) to yield implicit and full obedience to all the rules and regulations of the body; (3) community of goods so long as community of purpose; (4) teaching on the staunch Catholic principles; (5) preaching from place to place on circuits—route, mode, etc., to be determined by the bishop or by one authorized by him. We sincerely hope that you will find it your duty to join us. . . . I learn from Brother Adams that he has just written to our dear Brother Carey. How greatly we long after him, as a companion in our labors!"

A letter from this Brother Adams to Wadhams, directed, like that from Breck, to the General Seminary in Twentieth Street, New York City, is dated "December 6th, 1841." He begins by giving at some length a description of the country surrounding this new monastery; its beauty, its productions, and the character of its inhabitants. These latter he praises far above their neighbors of Illinois, Michigan, and Kentucky. "Nowhere have I seen any specimen of that vile animal that is called 'loafer' among them. . . . They have none of the Eastern prejudices against the church; they will listen to any sermon respectfully and with attention; not in the yawning, spitting, pick-tooth, boots-upon-the-bench sort of style and attitude in which your Kentuckian graces the house of God, but calmly and respectfully; and yet, mark you, my brother, a sermon, however strong it may be, or however pointed, will have as little effect upon these men as boiling water flung in the face of a marble statue. Sermons can make no impression."

The writer then proposes his remedy for this difficulty, which lies in an example of penance and self-mortification united to a "Catholic" churchmanship. He then urges his friend Wadhams as follows:

"Dear brother, if you can in almost every way deny yourself, can be content to remain unmarried for an indefinite period, to live on the coarsest food, to deny yourself the pleasure of cultivated society; then come to Wisconsin. . . . Whether you do come or no, in the name of God, and if you would not fall into many a perilous pit, begin a systematic course of self-denial, fasting upon the stationary days of the church. This is the only thing that will save a man from the legal spirit on the one side, and the luscious and animal spirit of religionism on the other.

If you want direction on this point, Carey will give it you. The spirit you see in him (what a spirit it is!) is the offspring of this practice."

Not long after his letter Adams visited our theological seminary in Twentieth Street; and many of us gathered around him, listening eagerly to his description of Nashotah, which seemed to us like a holy shrine set up amid the prairies, the nucleus of another Citeaux, with Breck for a St. Bernard. It must have increased very much from this small beginning. Nearly twenty years later three students from that institute visited me when I was officiating as parish priest in St. Peter's Church, Troy. They were tired of the kind of Catholicism they found at Nashotah, sincere though it was, and were resolved to become true Catholics. One, named McCurry, attached himself as priest to the diocese of Albany and was assigned to St. John's Church, in that city. The second is Father Henry L. Robinson, now rector at Chicopee, in the diocese of Springfield, Mass. The third convert was Graves, who, after finishing his studies, became connected with one of the Wisconsin dioceses. Nashotah is now, as I am informed, a flourishing seminary, receiving students from various parts of the United States. It is considered quite a conservative institution.

Whether Wadhams felt any inclination for this attempt at monastic life in Nashotah, I cannot say. Some others did—myself among the number. I endeavored, but without success, to persuade my father to transfer me to it from the seminary in New York. He took time to consider, and consulted Dr. Horatio Potter, then in charge of St. Peter's Church, Albany, but afterward Bishop of New York. The answer was unfavorable, Nashotah being represented as a nest where Catholic Protestants might be fledged into Catholics of the Roman type. My father gained still stronger impressions of danger from a Presbyterian clergyman, the famous Dr. Cox, formerly of Brooklyn. When asked what he thought of Puseyism, his answer was given in his own characteristic language: "Puseyism, sir, is the quintessence of the blackness of the darkness of the dark ages squirted into the nineteenth century." The doctor had some reason to speak in strong language. Puseyism had invaded his own household. He is said to have uttered his grief upon a public occasion in the following manner: "Hear, O Heavens! and give ear, O Earth! I have nourished and brought up children, and they have turned Episcopalians!"

Adams, the head of the school department at Nashotah, surrendered to Cupid in due time, marrying the daughter of Bishop Kemper. This was a great grief to Breck. The good prior, unable to cope with the "married influence," eventually turned his back on Nashotah and started a similar institution at Faribault, Minn. The fate against which he struggled followed him to this new plant also. Breck himself ere long got entangled matrimonially.

In all six students are known to have left Nashotah for the true fold at that time. Another convert in the immediate vicinity was the Rev. William Markoe, rector of St. John Chrysostom's Church. With him came his wife and his sister-in-law, who is now a nun.

I introduce next a precious letter from Arthur Carey, written after Wadhams had taken deacon's orders and was settled in Essex County. It was directed to Ticonderoga. Carey was looked upon at the seminary, both by professors and students, and by a host of others outside, as a sort of Saint Aloysius. His was, indeed, a beautiful and lovable character, and only a man like Wadhams could have secured and cemented a friendship so strong as that which existed between these two pure and fervent souls. We give the letter, therefore, as a memorial of both:

"NEW YORK, October 23d, '43.

"DEAREST WADHAMS: Do you recollect how happy I used to be when you tapped at my room door at the seminary, and I said 'Come in!' and in you came; and how I used to jump up to receive you, and how we used almost to hug each other; and how we sang together, and, horrible to tell, looked over the breviary together, and talked and laughed together; and how you abused my *pope*, on the door, and how I took his part, and how we discussed all the affairs of the church so wisely, and then adjourned and took a nice long walk, and so on? And now it is all over, and we are parted, and you are doing I know not what, and I am all alone in my room, writing to you, and feeling funny, queer, strange, a kind of blue feeling—do you know what I mean? I hope not, for it is very far indeed from pleasant; and yet I seem to wish you might occasionally feel blue, so as to sympathize with me, and to make you think over past times, that are gone forever, and are never coming back again. Think of that: Never coming back again! No, never! I have a good deal, or at least a little, news to tell you, but it seems so natural to run on in this old-fashioned, loose way that I hardly like to stop it. Does it remind you of old times? Does it make you think of those times, when you used to visit me and eat brown bread and sit before the fire? Or, are you now too parsonical for these seminary reminiscences? It is cruel even to hint that you have got above those times, when I know perfectly well that you have not, and that you will not in a hurry—I mean that you *never* will. Will you ever? Will you ever, Wadhams? Ah, why do not you answer? Why do not you say, 'No, never!' and pacify me? Why do not you speak? But, poor me! it is not your fault; you can't speak to me when you are so far away, can you? If you could, you would, would not you? Wouldn't you try and make me laugh now, and cheer me up a bit, if you were here? Yes, to be sure you would, like a good fellow as you are, ain't you? This is something like the way we used to run on together, I think; but I must stop it now and begin to be serious. And to begin, I must beg ten thousand pardons for forgetting so shamefully to leave the *Critic* for you to take with you. I have been thinking ever since that I would send it by post, but my brother tells me it would cost you *a dollar* in postage. Tell me what I am to do, and it shall immediately be attended to. If you tell me to send this one by post, I shall conclude you will wish me to continue and send them all the same way; unless you say to the contrary. Pardon me for my carelessness. And now about myself. I am engaged as Dr. Seabury's assistant. His vestry renewed their call immediately after the convention, and as the bishop urged me strongly to accept it, I have done so for six months. The salary is five hundred dollars per annum—quite enough to support me, but no more. I am lodging at 101 Charlton Street, quite near the church. I preach on Sunday afternoons, and open the church for Wednesday and Friday services, morning and evening, and saints' day services. I was afraid to begin with daily services, and the doctor thought better not at present. He says I may do anything I please, and he will never interfere with me, but always support me, which is pleasant, at all events. Dr. Sherwood, of Hyde Park, gave me a book (which I must lend you, as soon as I see you) by old Dr. Smith, of Connecticut. It is very interesting indeed. Its title is *Primitive Psalmody*, and he maintains that chanting is the only canonical ecclesiastical music; that metre psalm-singing is an abomination, and that metre hymns are only to be tolerated. He is very warm, quite eloquent, and rather learned; he is extremely severe on the Puritans and Calvinist party, and wonderfully polite and reverential toward the Church of Rome. He was himself a very good musician. He was a Scotchman, and came over with Bishop Seabury. Dr. Sherwood was his pupil, and he is a churchman of the very highest grade and an admirer of the O. [Oxford] Tracts and the *British Critic*, of which he is a 'constant reader.' Please direct to me, at my lodgings, when you write, and this you must *soon* and *frequently* do, and I will endeavor, as I can, to answer you. Isn't Bishop McIlvaine cutting some strange capers? He will do mischief yet, before he stops; it is impossible to say what he may not do, if he once makes up his mind to it; but I doubt whether he carries any great weight out of his own diocese. The laity and clergy cannot really do much harm in our church, because they can never carry anything against the bishops; I suppose the bishops can always carry their own dioceses; but on the other hand, the bishops may do almost any

amount of harm, if they be once opposed to each
other. Our diocesan organization enables each
bishop to separate his own diocese, in effect, from
all others; and so we may place ourselves in a position of relative schism, and eventually break up
our general convention. McMaster is now sitting
by my side; he has just come down from the
seminary, and is now reading to me out of the
October number of the *British Critic*. He sends
his best love to you.

"Yours ever in all brotherly love,
"A. CAREY."

The active religious zeal fermenting in the
minds of the more fervent students at the General Seminary, and looking forward to future
work, extended itself in two directions. There
was much interest in foreign missions. Some
took a special interest in China and the Eastern
countries of Asia. Others were more interested
in Bishop Southgate's efforts to establish an
unity between Anglicanism and the ancient
schismatic Greek churches. Not that these students looked upon the Eastern churches as schismatic, for that would have placed themselves in
the same category; but there was a feeling that
the nearer Anglicans, with their "apostolical succession," could be made to harmonize with the
various Greek churches, the more appearance of
real unity they would present in the face of that
great church whose centre was at Rome, but

whose circumference encloses all nations and all ages.

A missionary society was existing at the seminary and was in a flourishing state. There was a class of students, however, in whose minds there was a strong yearning for what in the Catholic Church is called "the religious life;" meaning not merely a general aspiration toward Christian perfection, but embracing those special means to this end which consist in a mingling of community life with a seclusion from the world. It is hard, nevertheless, for an earnest American mind, however much it may long for internal purification and sanctification, to divest itself of the thought of active work for others, and therefore, in the mind of Wadhams and men of his own type, the highest ideal of a Christian ministry naturally took the form of a community of missionaries bound to poverty, chastity, and obedience. The institute at Nashotah was an honest and earnest attempt at this; and no wonder that so many eyes at the New York seminary were fixed upon that land of lakes and prairies. New York State, however, had its wilderness in the North Woods, of which Essex County formed a part. There, immediately upon his ordination, was stationed Edgar P. Wadhams. There he was already doing missionary work, with a heart yearning after perfection. This pointed him out as a natural centre round whom others might gather. What has just been said will make the following letter seem both natural and intelligible. Henry McVickar, the writer, had been a fellow-seminarian with Wadhams, was a classmate of my own, was familiar and in active sympathy with both. Let me also say of him here, briefly but emphatically, that he was a most fervent soul of rare endowments, and a Christian gentleman of the most perfect type.

His letter to Wadhams, directed to Ticonderoga from Chelsea, bears the date of August 30th, 1844. It must be understood that "Chelsea" was then the name for that part of New York City in which is situated the General Seminary, at the corner of Ninth Avenue and Twentieth Street. The letter was, therefore, written in McVickar's room at the seminary. After some previous matter, which for brevity's sake I omit, he launched into the subject which was uppermost in his mind in the following words:

"Walworth and myself have been plotting against your freedom all the morning, and as I don't feel easy I propose to confess the whole truth to you—which is this, that we propose offering our assistance in transforming you into a monk, *Frater* or *Pater*, whichever may seem best.

"Mr. Dyer's death (what a blow it must have been to you! I can well feel) has opened the Essex County mission so that it may be put upon a new and better footing (I speak under correction). You may remember some conversation we had together before you left here, in which you expressed the opinion that you might find one or two young men, desirous of preparing for the ministry, who would live with you and form the nucleus of such an institution as Nashotah. I wish to remind you of the idea you then brought out. I confess it struck me very much at the time, and has been a hope next my heart ever since.

"Can anything be done to realize it? Are you inclined to it? Will Judge B—— back you? If so, let me know; when it will be needed I will provide some more backing. In the mean time I can offer you a coadjutor after your own warm heart—Walworth, . . . who finds himself unable on account of his eyes to proceed with the seminary course. . . . Inclination would lead him to Breck, but in compliance with his father's wishes he gives that up, and he now looks to your quarter. He could *lay-read and teach*, with a moderate use of his eyes. . . . I have seen some late letters from Breck, by which he appears to be prospering. Although he is the only clergyman, he has among his students some five lay-readers, and thus supplies twelve or thirteen stations every Sunday, and finds his efficiency far greater than he could have expected.

"Walworth proposes to come and see you in September—say the fourteenth; meanwhile he will be here; and we should like to hear from you in the interval."

It seems very probable that even at this early date Wadhams' mind had been visited by strong misgivings as to the character of the church to which he was attached—whether he could safely trust himself in it as being in any true sense a branch of the church of Christ. There is a passage in this letter which evidently shows that McVickar believed him to be troubled with misgivings of this kind. The passage refers to some previous letter of Wadhams':

"I fear your rainy sky in Essex makes you low-spirited. . . . I had intended to urge you to give up the idea of the possibility of your leaving the *mother who begot you to God*, but I cannot bring myself to believe that you will ever leave an altar on which lies the body of Our Lord while life is in you.

"Whatever is true we have a right to believe and act upon, but always with prudence, tempering truth with mercy, 'Jesus with Mary.'

"It was very kind of you to write, and I shall long to hear from you again. I beg the benefit of your prayers at the 'offering of the Salutary Host,' and remain,

"Yours most sincerely,
"HENRY MCVICKAR."

Shortly after the above letter Wadhams came down to New York, and upon his return to his mission took me with him. On our way north we visited McMaster, at Hyde Park, and the

Rev. Mr. Wheaton, at Poughkeepsie. McMaster was full of advanced ideas and disposed to rally us both as slow-coaches. When driving one day from Hyde Park to Poughkeepsie, as we passed an Episcopal church McMaster called out suddenly: "What are you taking your hat off to, Wadhams? To that old meeting-house? There's nothing inside of that but a communion table, where the vestrymen put their hats. Wait till you come to a real church with a real altar and a sacrifice."

We did not find Mr. Wheaton at home, but visited the church in which he then officiated as assistant. While standing outside the chancel our advanced friend said: "There are four sacraments administered in this church, if any at all." "Baptism, the Lord's Supper, and Confirmation," said Wadhams; "that makes three; but what is the fourth?" "Why, Penance," said McMaster. "Do you see that chair inside the railing? That's where Wheaton sat when I made my confession to him. It was something new for him and he didn't want to do it, but I insisted upon it; and didn't I frighten the life out of him!" Years afterward it was a pleasure to meet Dr. Wheaton when he had become a Catholic.

Wadhams and I proceeded from thence to Ticonderoga, the trip from Troy to Whitehall being made on the canal. After a few weeks I was obliged to return to New York to consult my oculist. From there McVickar and I addressed a joint letter, or rather two letters on the same sheet, to our friend at Ticonderoga. Mine runs as follows:

"DEAR FATHER EDGAR: If this epistle should be too brief, charge my eyes with the offence. I don't know where to direct it to, but trust it will find you at Ti. I will be ready to come back to Wadhams Mills just as soon as you wish me. . . . Please write me immediately. . . . Say what books you would have me purchase. McV—— has just given me a check for $50 for tools, books, etc. I shall purchase all the Lives of Saints, breviaries, and two or three manuals of devotion; what more would you like in the way of books or else? Can the cooking-stove, shovel and tongs, beds, bedding, etc., be obtained best in Essex Co.? Shall I bring writing paper, etc.? We are, I think, all three ready (*i.e.*, willing) for action. May God and Our Lady prosper us! My love to Judge B——, etc. . . .
"Yours faithfully forever,
"CLA. W."

This is McVickar's letter:

"November 6th, 1844.
"MY DEAR WADHAMS: Walworth's return last Saturday gave me the greatest satisfaction. I had missed his sympathy more than I could have suspected I should, and I can appreciate better

than before the comfort you will be to one another this winter.

"Any plans you shall adopt I shall subscribe as the best, only I would have you consider this winter as one of trial, and on that account perhaps, as well as others, we should practise the doctrine of reserve; consider the mighty game we are playing, and how sure we ought to be of our moves before we make them; but in all these matters you are a far better judge than I am, and I am ashamed (if it were not an evidence of the interest I take) of my self-sufficiency.

"I hear that they want to call McMaster to Fishkill, if the bishop will ordain him; but the bishop is so full of his own matters (having been presented for trial for immoral conduct) that he cannot bestow much thought upon Mac, who has had a severe trial. Our turns may not be very far distant.

"The *Lives of the English Saints* I am delighted with, and would not part with them upon any consideration.

"Could you not manage to pick up some orphan child this winter belonging to no one (the younger the better), over whom you might exercise complete control? They are the stuff we must in a great measure depend upon. As my letter is made up of patches, I will end it by an extract [from] Ward's book which may point out the course 'the Apostolicals' in England would advise: 'However, the one method that carries

God's blessing with it of reforming a bad system is first of all to load the existing framework with all possible good, if it will bear it well; if not, God himself has solved for us the question and the system breaks down with no direct agency of ours' (p. 368).

"Your promised letter I shall expect with great anxiety, and I shall feel authorized hereafter to apply to you for guidance in any difficulties into which I may fall, and shall ever remain, with the sincerest love,

"Yours truly,
"HENRY McVICKAR."

All the earnestness and hopefulness with which we three aspirants after monasticism set to work to realize our vision is to be seen in our purchase of breviaries and other books for prayer and pious reading, and of tools for manual labor, for we believed, with St. Bernard and his Cistercians, that good monks must labor as well as pray. That hope was very high in our hearts may be seen from the fact that Wadhams and McVickar made their wills to secure a sort of endowment for the institute. I, who had no other property but myself either in possession or in prospect, had only myself to bequeath, and I did it with a will. We had even fixed upon a name for our "Clairvaux," which was to be called St. Mary's, and our minds were sometimes occupied in designing cloisters. I have no personal recollection of

McMaster as included in our proposed community. It would seem, however, from the following letter (written in 1844, and mailed from Hyde Park, N. Y.), that he had offered himself to Wadhams for some kind of a combination which was to be cemented by vows:

"IN FESTO O SAPIENTIA, Dec. 16.
"MY DEAR WADHAMS: I would have written to you long ago, but I was determined you should keep your word and write first, as in duty bound. I am delighted to hear how well you are coming on; things seem to be nearer what you would wish than you could have hoped a few months ago. I am sorry you did not write a week earlier than you did, for then I would have had time to make this letter twice as long as it will be now. However, if you answer it soon, I will write a longer one soon after the holidays. I spend next week in town, and am full of business in the mean while. I have had two letters from England, within the month; one from Dalgairns, the other from Oakeley. Both are very kind and interesting. Oakeley cannot immediately go on with St. Bernard; his intimate friend and coadjutor, who was to have assisted him, has *crossed* and is gone. O—— says he has no intention of following him at present. He thinks the step (which was taken without consulting friends) was owing to morbid excitement of mind and peculiar circumstances. He means as soon as he

can to resume his labors on St. Bernard. Dalgairns is full of the state of parties consequent on the recent election of V. Chancellor, and, like Oakeley, writes in bad spirits. The breach is irreparable between the thorough-paced ones and the Hook party, and this seems to discourage them. Ward's book they speak of in the highest terms. Of course an attempt is being made by some in authority to get hold of him and punish him, but this is not likely to succeed. He is coming out in a new edition in two volumes, enlarged from the first. Of the lives of the saints, St. Augustine is by Oakeley; Sts. Wolstan and William, by Mr. Church (a fellow of Oriel and follower of Mr. Newman, author of the articles on St. Anselm in the *B. Critic*); Sts. Paulinus, Bega, etc., constituting No. VI., is by F. W. Faber, the poet. I am rejoiced to see him so true a man; he *talks* harder than any one of them, and I think from several things that he has recovered very much from his self-conceit, which used so to spoil his writings. Dalgairns leads me to infer that he himself is the author of St. Stephen and St. Gilbert, being Nos. I. and VII.; finally some of the shorter of the *Legends of the Hermit Saints* are by Newman. Have you all these? I see No. VIII. announced, and volume vi. of the *Plain Sermons*.

"You ask very kindly about my own affairs. I know little about them *externally*. That Fishkill business is all nonsense; they would not think of me. To tell the truth, I am very careless about taking orders. I believe a furious storm is gathering, and will very soon drive us to Rome. The only possible alternative is the breaking up of our communion between different dioceses. Whether that could save us, considering the reckless character of the Whitting-*hamites*—or, as I am disposed henceforth to call them, the 'Hamites,' as if from the father of Canaan the accursed—whether such a division can save us, is, I say, very doubtful. I think our present tack is a deep love for our church—of course for her poor remnant of Catholicism, which remnant we as dutiful sons will strive to preserve and increase. I think we may well *express* ourselves strongly both in the way of affection for her and of deep consciousness that she has forfeited almost everything, and may very shortly forfeit the rest, which we are striving to prevent. I think, however, that it is most likely when we openly avow belief in the unity of the church as consisting in communion with St. Peter's chair, and in communion of saints as implying, or rather including, invocation of them, that they will stop their ears and hurl us out. I shall have a good deal to say to you when I return from the city. I am going to urge Seabury, furiously, to advance his colors, and take a bold stand in the *Churchman*. I wrote him a week ago a letter that I dare say has frightened him a little, and I mean to frighten him still more. If we stay, as we want to, in our church, we stay to work and to *talk*, not to be quiet. And this must and shall be allowed us; and so I told him. (By the way, he spoke very highly of you a few weeks ago when I was in town, and expressed regret that he never could get hold of you.) I must thank you for offering me a retreat at St. Mary's. There is nothing to keep me from joining you in the spring, so far as I am concerned; but it will not do to make schemes. I feel that hitherto I have done nothing to fit myself for what may be in store for us. My wretched want of humility has spoiled me in everything, and now, if now indeed, gives me everything to do yet. If I am ordained in the spring, which may be, cannot you come down? I speak only on conjecture, but there are several who will be likely to urge it. I have gone every length with Mr. Wheaton, and he goes with us heartily. Oh, if his wife was only in a convent! He is very religious and earnest, I assure you, in spite of his wife. When have you heard from Shepherd? Wadhams, I want to see a common rule adopted by us, whether living together or not, to be observed strictly. It must be general, but include regular canonical hours, celibacy by vow, and obedience to the superior of the 'order,' if we may so call it. Let it not surprise you when I say I am free to take these vows. Don't say so to any one. I cannot explain farther. To these, of course, confession must be added—oh! how I long to see it established with us, for my own sake. Platt wrote me lately from Rochester, and expressed a great wish to see you. He finds it hard work with those nasty High-Churchmen. I wish he was in this diocese. So say I of every one that is right-minded: Concentrate first, and go forth thence.

"Thank you for *Spooner's Sermon;* there are good things in it, but he is crochety and out of joint. He deals harder with others than with himself, I fancy, or he would be more religious in his tone. Have you seen *Questions for Self-Examination*, republished in Albany, under auspices of Williams & Potter, of Albany?

"I am glad Walworth is contented. Remember me kindly to him. I tried to see him when in town, but could not find him. Write me very soon, and a long letter. The details of your doings interested me much. Believe me ever most sincerely, Yours, etc.,

"B. B. J. McMaster."

The Oxford Movement, so called, was now fast coming to a crisis, both in England and in America. In June, 1844, William George Ward, of Balliol College, Oxford, published his celebrated *Ideal of a Christian Church*. This ideal was so plainly contrary to the actual Anglican Church, so radically different, in truth, that it produced a general horror in the minds of average churchmen, and no small dismay in the ranks even of Tractarians. To borrow a simile of Dr. New-

Ogdensburg City Hospital and Orphan Asylum.

man, the result was like that produced by "Sindbad the Sailor" and his companions when they kindled a cooking-fire on the back of a barren little island. The experiment changed the island into a whale. The sluggish animal first shivered, then threw his tail high up in the air and relieved himself speedily both of the coals and the cooks. In Oxford a prosecution was soon initiated to condemn Ward and deprive him of his degrees. Affairs at the Twentieth Street seminary drew on toward a crisis at the same time. The American whale also woke up and prepared to dive, and the first that fell into the water were certain Catholicizing seminarians, who happened to be where the coals were hottest. The hard-fisted old Knickerbocker bishop, who was president of the seminary and had hitherto been their protector, had come into disgrace and was unable to give any efficient help. The High-Church bishops of the "Catholic" kind were made feeble through fear, and those of the Low-Church grew correspondingly bold and clamorous. What followed at the seminary is sufficiently developed in a letter from McVickar to Wadhams, dated at the seminary, December 31st, 1844. The first few lines of the letter we omit. They refer to architectural plans for the new "St. Mary's" at Wadhams Mills.

" . . . An affair in which Walworth is interested, and of which, if report says true, he has already heard of from his bishop, is keeping the seminary in hot water." (This was a mistake so far as to any communication between Bishop De Lancey and myself.) "The history is this. About two weeks ago Mr. Ogilby sent for Watson (m. class) and told him that he had been informed that there was an organized party in and out of the seminary, including clergy, for Romanizing the church. Donnelly, Taylor, Watson, Platt, Walworth, and myself belonged to it. He questioned Watson on his views, and W—— acknowledged that he used prayers to the saints and considered the Church of England schismatical. As soon as we heard it, we (Donnelly, Taylor, and myself) called on Mr. O—— and asked him what he had heard against us and who had informed him. He refused to answer, and asked us to answer some of his questions, which we refused to do, and he reported us all to our bishops. D—— and I had seen Bishop O——, who says he is satisfied; but the faculty have taken it up, and I am to appear before them on the 7th *proximo* on the charge of recommending Romish books, and also on the charge of believing in the papal supremacy. The information comes through P——, whom I think Walworth knew, and who has used the basest deception to get information. Whatever happens it will make no difference in my remaining in the P. E. Church. We call ourselves Catholic. I may, therefore, hold all Catholic truths, which I am determined to do.

"Whicher is here, and gives out that he is sent for by his bishop. I think that Platt may be down also.

"A letter has lately appeared by Mr. Oakeley giving his reasons to a Roman Catholic for remaining in the Church of England. It is said to be a very thorough thing. The reports of Mr. Newman's having gone to the Church of Rome are all false. Mr. Forbes is getting on astonishingly well, and Dr. Seabury's sermons are noble in doctrine and power; but Mr. Wheaton of Po'keepsie, under Mr. McMaster's guidance, is becoming the staunchest priest in the church. So we have no reason to despair, and if we did not meet with trouble we should want one mark of holding the true faith. Remember me kindly to Walworth, etc."

Chapter III.

A Storm at Oxford Echoed at the Chelsea Seminary.—Sindbad's Whale Flops.—The Cloister Goes Under.—Friends Cross Over to Rome.

1845.

ON the 13th of February, 1845, a convocation of the University of Oxford condemned William George Ward's *Ideal of a Christian Church*, as containing passages inconsistent with the Thirty-nine Articles, and deprived him of his degrees in the university. Mr. Ward was not only a clergyman in priest's orders, but a fellow of Balliol College and had been professor of mathematics at that college. Of course, this blow, aggressive and decisive as it was, fell not only upon him, but upon a large number of others who stood in the same position with him. When the convocation broke up and passed out into the street, Mr. Ward was cheered by the undergraduates, and the vice-chancellor was saluted with hisses and snowballs from the same quarter. To borrow a most truthful and forcible expression already applied to these proceedings, "the university was ostracising half its most promising sons."

It must, however, be acknowledged that the Anglican Church, notwithstanding her enormous latitude of doctrine, was too thoroughly Protestant in spirit to hold such men as Ward. And on the other hand, a large number of Puseyites were too much puffed up with the fancy of being Catholic for him to sympathize any longer with them.

"A Catholic priest at Old Hall College was put somewhat out of countenance when, in answer to his rather sneering remark, 'I suppose you *call* yourself a Catholic, Mr. Ward,' he received the reply, 'Oh dear no! You are a Catholic, I am a Puseyite.' He did not believe himself to be a priest, or to have the power of forgiving sins. . . . And when once a friend said to him, 'Bear in mind that you are, on our principles, really a priest of God,' Ward broke off the discourse by saying, 'If that is the case, the whole thing is infernal humbug.'"

The University of Oxford is a far more ancient and venerable institution than the Church of England, and far more vigorous with real English life. It has more of a mind of its own, it has more liberty to speak, and its word goes farther among English churchmen. This it is that made Ward's condemnation so crushing a blow to all would-be Catholics. It was still possible for men belonging to the "movement" to remain in the university and in the church on condition of keeping their mouths shut, but these men said in their hearts, to use the words of McMaster's letter already quoted, "If we stay, as we want to, in our church, we stay to work and to *talk*, not to be quiet." By keeping this in mind the reader will easily understand that by the above act of convocation the Oxford movement had practically come to a collapse. What was true of the Church of England was also true of her affectionate little daughter on this side of the water. Ward retired from Balliol and from Oxford, Oakeley resigned his charge at Margaret Chapel, London, in the following summer, and Newman did not hesitate to intimate to his friends that he was no longer at peace in the church of his birth. In this country also a crisis had come. Several seminarians were, upon complaint, subjected to an informal trial at the Twentieth Street seminary.

What interested Wadhams in a very special manner was that Henry McVickar, a prospective member of our little monastery, feeling crowded out by the result, withdrew to rooms at Columbia College. The Protestant Episcopal Church was no longer a home for many earnest souls. The test contained in McVickar's letter of November 6th, 1844, already given, for "reforming a bad system," had been applied and failed. Her framework would not bear that load "of all possible good," which they had attempted to put upon it. Enthusiastic young men might still be allowed to play Catholic, but they must not presume to mean anything by it. McVickar, though much discouraged, still seemed to hope something from the monastic idea, though he gradually grew more non-committal until finally he withdrew. His next letter to the prior of St. Mary's, dated at Columbia College, February 23d, 1845, reads as follows:

"MY DEAR WADHAMS: I received your welcome letter a few days back and have sent a bundle as directed. You cannot tell how I regret not being able to send you Ward's book, but when Adams left here I promised that a copy should be sent to Nashotah, and if I could not get any one else to send it I would send my own, which I soon expect to have an opportunity of doing. I shall, however, try and get you a sight of the book before long. As to its being published I can only say I hope for it. Mr. Johnson of Brooklyn offers, I understand, to take twenty-five copies if the Appletons will put out an edition.

"Speaking of Mr. J——, some of the students whom I have seen tell me that about fifteen of them were over there yesterday (Saturday) to chant the Psalter for him and are to go again on Easter eve.

"In a letter to Walworth I have mentioned some of the reasons that led me to take the step I took at the seminary. At the time I felt very much the need of advice, but those upon whose judgment I would have placed the most confidence were absent; and what I did had to be done quickly and some protest seemed necessary. And, indeed, I was more restricted by the action which was taken than you seem to suppose; perhaps I made too great concessions—I allowed that I was not the judge of what was injurious to the seminary, but I conceded that the faculty were, and that if they would point out how they thought I had injured it I would avoid it for the future. This they did in a general way, but so as to restrict me more than I thought right; but if I had remained at the seminary I should have submitted to it and thought it my duty to do so. But I was free to leave the institution, and I did so.

". . . No. 8 of the Lives of the Saints is one of the most thorough of the series. McMaster supposes it to be Mr. Newman, and he is a good judge of style.

"McMaster has not been very well this winter. When last I heard from him he was cogitating a successor for Bishop O——. . . .

"I have had a long letter from Johnson, who has advanced astonishingly—developed, perhaps I had better say. I wish you or Walworth would write to him, and urge him to come into this diocese. I regard him as a most valuable man.

"Mr. Kneeland is my room-mate at present, and is studying theology with an energy that would shame most students. He has just finished Ward, and Moehler [on "Symbolism"], and is delighted with them.

"I saw Mr. Carey the other evening. His accounts from his son Henry (Arthur Carey's brother), who is in Madeira, are far from encouraging; his heart appears very much affected. Give my best love to Walworth, and believe me,

"Very truly and sincerely yours,
"Henry McVickar."

The letter that follows needs no introduction.

"New York, Maundy Thursday, 1845.

"My dear Wadhams: . . . To begin with the question which concerns me most intimately, you ask: When and whether I will join you? To this I reply, it depends upon my obtaining orders. If I do, with the bishop's permission, I will join you as deacon immediately afterwards. To join you as a layman is a question I have never considered. My present judgment is against it. Now, I wish to be very explicit in this matter with you.

"I am extremely doubtful whether I can obtain orders without exciting new commotions and troubles; and if I think so when the time comes *I shall not apply for them. You must therefore act without counting upon or regarding me in this matter.*

"My three years' candidateship (till the expiration of which the bishop tells me I cannot be ordained) does not expire till some time toward the end of November next.

"Under these circumstances I do not think it right that I should control in the least your movements. In order, therefore, to render your action as free as possible and that you may act for the best, *I accept the release you have given me so far as to avoid the trust under your will, and desire you to revoke it, or destroy the will as soon as convenient.* This does not in the slightest interfere in the establishment of the house, if you wish to do so, and at the same time simplifies matters and renders you freer to choose the best course.

"With this statement as to myself I must leave you and Walworth to decide the other questions, and upon your own course. I am glad Walworth has been engaged in so useful a work as preparing a book of devotions, and hereby offer my subscription for half a dozen copies at the least, or as many more as he sets me down for. The warmest inquiries are made after him by the students that I meet at the Annunciation.*

"The news from England is important. Ward is deprived of his degree and fellowship. . . . Remember me affectionately to W——, and if he is harassed with doubts, believe me there are many who sympathize with him. With a deep interest in all that concerns you, I remain, ever yours faithfully,

"HENRY MCVICKAR."

---

* Dr. Seabury's old church, where Carey had been assistant, situated at the corner of Prince and Thompson Streets.—C. A. W.

It ought to be easy for the reader to understand that this period was to Wadhams one of great mental anxiety and sometimes anguish of heart. This, however, did not keep the young deacon from faithful and hard labor in the field of his mission. I was eye-witness only to a small part of this, as I remained in Wadhams Mills during his frequent absences, officiating as lay-reader and catechist there on Sundays when he held service at Ticonderoga and Port Henry. I can say little, therefore, of his work and way of working, except what I saw him do at Wadhams Mills. I do not think any of his people at the Mills were sick that winter. He had opportunities, however, to show kindness to sick people not of his fold. I left him once at the village inn to keep night watch over a man suddenly taken ill, under circumstances which caused great alarm. I left him stretched out on three chairs beside the sick-bed. His weight rested chiefly upon a central chair; his feet reposed upon another, and his head was supported on a third, which was tilted up on two legs. He was accustomed to this way of couching and always said he never slept better than in that fashion. I heard the sick man whisper to a friend who happened in, "Isn't he a good fellow!" A young man whose apartments were right over the village store was taken with the small-pox. The villagers were filled with alarm and would none of them come near him. Even the village doctor came only once, and then covered from neck to foot with a long bag, something like a night-gown, made expressly for the purpose. The young man's family, only four miles distant, kept away from him, except his step-mother, who came to carry him home as soon as he was well enough to be moved. The village store beneath him was closed up, and a farmer who lived across the street was so frightened that I saw him once shaking his fist at the house when he saw the door opened opposite to him. Wadhams, however, was in and out frequently, and so was his good mother, who brought food for the patient. She took no precaution for herself, only she was careful to send two grandchildren home. It was decided by the villagers that for the public safety the young man should be removed to a deserted and dilapidated hut in the neighborhood; but, it being the dead of winter, neither Wadhams nor his mother would listen to this; and, since the authorities could find no one willing to undertake the job of removal, the project was abandoned.

Wadhams preached every Sunday afternoon, alternating between Ticonderoga, Port Henry, and Wadhams Mills. The reader may be interested to know what his sermons were like at this time and how he delivered them. I recall one occasion when he preached in the school-house at Ticonderoga. He inveighed against lazy postures in devotion, and spoke of men who would not kneel for fear of getting dust on their knees, etc. The only person of this kind present was the leading gentleman of his congregation, who sat directly under the preacher's desk, and saw the commanding form of our friend looking down upon him, not more than six feet distant, and emphasizing him most earnestly with his eyes. This gentleman's respect for the young apostle was, nevertheless, too great to allow him to take offence. We both took supper with him that evening, and the conversation was as cordial on all sides as if nothing but abstract truth had been uttered in the morning sermon.

It is well to remark here that Wadhams took no pride in his own utterances. In the commencement he wrote out all his sermons, and that carefully. Still he was ready to read from printed books any sermon that pleased him, or anything that would serve his purpose when short of matter. In one same day at Ticonderoga he used manuscript sermons of mine and McMaster's, one in the morning and one in the afternoon. They were exercise sermons which we had written in New York and preached before the class. Both of us were in the audience, and we were astonished and delighted to see how much he made of them with his strong emphasis and earnest manner. He had read the sermons carefully beforehand, and prepared himself well to do justice to them. He was less cautious on another occasion at Wadhams Mills, and felt himself caught in a trap. His *repertoire* of sermons was exhausted and hard work during the week had prevented him from making any preparation. "Walworth," said he, "I want one of your seminary sermons; I'm short."

"All right," I said; "I'll lend you one; but I never preached it at the seminary, and you may not like it."

"I've no time to read it," said he, "and I'll take it on trust."

The sermon was on the "Infallibility of the Church." It was rather a heavy gun, and would have excited much astonishment if used in Twentieth Street before the professor in class. I watched my friend as he delivered it, and not without some fear of the consequences. The audience showed no signs of agitation or dissatisfaction. Wadhams himself, however, grew red in the face as he proceeded, and I noticed that whenever he came to some terrible words about "the Rock of Peter," which often occurred, he braced himself up, and pounded the desk with unusual energy. After the morning service was over, and the Sunday-school exercises also—for which all the audience remained—I conducted his mother, widow Wadhams, to her house, where our rooms were, and waited with some apprehension for my friend's return. When he entered the room he glared at me for a little while, and then said, with a remarkable mildness: "I tell you what, my very dear Christian friend, if I had known what was in that sermon I wouldn't have preached it." "Well," I said, "if you are satisfied, I am sure the congregation is. Nobody here will take any exception to anything you preach."

In this, however, I was mistaken. In the evening we visited a cousin of his, an Episcopalian, whose husband, however, was a Baptist. He said to me: "I liked the sermon this morning very much, but there was one thing in it which I couldn't exactly take in. I don't see how you Episcopalians can prove the infallibility of the Pope." The sermon, of course, was not intended to carry the point of infallibility so far. Nevertheless, I let this odd mistake pass, not being altogether unpleased with it.

"You cannot?" said I, "why the thing is not so very difficult! Just look at the Scriptures," and I proceeded to present some arguments drawn from Scripture and from reason, arguments which at this very time were leading me rapidly to the Catholic faith. The preacher of the morning said nothing, but looked amazed.

The objector still objected, but the good lady, his wife, was disposed to stand firmly by any doctrine that seemed to come from the pulpit or the general seminary.

"Hush!" said she to her husband, "don't talk so much; you only show your ignorance." It is hard to say precisely how much of the confiding simplicity of Wadhams' flock was owing to anything else than his own magnetic sincerity.

Following these events and the communications from McVickar already given, there came a correspondence between him and myself which led to a distinct abandonment by him of our monastic scheme, a consequent termination of my residence with Wadhams, and to a termination, also, of my connection with the Protestant Episcopal Church. In truth, my state of mind was very much like that of Ward and Oakeley in England.

I had little confidence in the validity of Anglican orders. I felt myself to be in a state of schism, separated from the ancient and true Church of Christ. Moreover, whatever toleration was given by Anglicanism to Catholic ideas, rank heresy received far more efficient toleration; and I saw little hope of reviving a breathless corpse by our weak efforts to blow a little wind into its nostrils. I began to realize that, whatever of supernatural life there was in individual Anglicans, they did not derive it from Anglicanism. The condition of Wadhams' mind was very similar to my own. Even the fragmentary correspondence of that time now in my possession contains warnings from his friends which, if my remembrance serves, were never communicated to me. I think he was afraid of adding to my uneasiness, and his own soul was not in a mood that made him capable of reassuring friends. At one time, when there was some reason to apprehend serious danger from sickness, I said to him:

"My dear old fellow, if this thing should turn out badly I shall want better help than you can give me." "Never fear," he answered; "in that case you shall have a priest, and it shall be some one that *is* a priest for certain."

The correspondence between McVickar and myself above referred to contained expressions on my part of distrust in Episcopalianism and longing aspirations after unity with Rome which alarmed my friend in New York. These expressions drew from him declarations of a determination to abide in the church where he was at all hazards, and of an inability to co-operate practically with any whose hearts were already in another fold. The crisis had come. Sindbad's island whale was unmistakably in motion. She would not endure any more hot coals. The presumptuous sailors who had been dancing on her back were now obliged to look out for their own safety. It had become necessary either to go under with the whale or to strike out for a safer refuge. To particularize: St. Mary's Monastery in the North Woods had turned out to be a vision. That vision had vanished, and in its place was left nothing but a roofless log house on the Wadhams farm. The following note will now speak for itself:

"Your Study, May 5th, 1845.

"Dear Wadhams: In a few minutes I shall be gone—and oh, as I lean my breast against your stand, how wildly something beats within.

It seems as if I were about to separate from everything I love, and my poor heart, faithless and unconscientious, wants to be left behind among the Protestants. I am not manly enough to make a stout Catholic; but it is a great privilege to be a weak one. Well, do not you forget me. Indeed you cannot—you have been such a good, kind, elder brother to me, you would not be able if you tried to forget me. When hereafter you speak of me, speak freely of me for truth's sake, with all my faults; but when you think of me alone, try to forget all that is bad for love's sake, and although your imagination should in this way create a different person, no matter, so you call it by my name. We have stormy times before us, dear W——; but may God grant us the privilege to ride the storm *together*. Farewell until we meet again, and *when* and *where* shall that be?

"'Lead Thou us on!'

"C. W."

In close connection with the above note is the copy of a letter from Wadhams to McVickar. The original was carried to New York City by McMaster. He had come up to visit us at Ticonderoga, and we had arranged together, McMaster and I, to enter the Catholic Church, and for this purpose to apply to the Redemptorist Fathers at their house in Third Street, New York. I went on first, leaving him to follow me after finishing his visit at Ticonderoga.

It is a noticeable fact that Wadhams should have made and preserved a copy of this one letter among so many which he wrote. No doubt he felt that it marked the turn of a great tide in his life. The letter reads as follows:

"CHURCH OF THE CROSS, TICONDEROGA,
"Tuesday in Whitsun Week, 1845.
"MY DEAR MCVICKAR: Conscious of great neglect to you, I now sit down after again returning to this place to answer your last kind letter.

"I cannot well describe to you the feelings that Walworth's note—written after I left him and left upon my table—has excited. Of him, his worth and advantage to me for the past months I need not speak to you who know him better than I and consequently know what they must have been. Every one regrets that he has left these mountains, particularly Judge and Mrs. B——, and the Hammonds at the Falls. Poor fellow! he suffered very much from his eyes during the winter and spring, and, after it was finally settled that we were not to have your company up here, became discontented. What step he has now taken you, doubtless, know better than I do. Though sorry that he has left me alone among these mountains, I am not sorry that I have a friend among the Roman Catholics. On the contrary, I am glad, for there is no knowing how soon we all may be obliged to leave our present communion—'that dispensation of God

which has been to all of us so great a blessing'
—and go to the church which is Catholic. I say
this, not expecting to abuse the kindness which
he and other friends may extend to me there,
but to express my thankfulness to them for their
manliness and straightforwardness. We are certainly under obligations to them for opening and
showing the way for those Americans that may
follow. It seems to be a conceded point now
among those who are leading the way in our
church that the Church of Rome has all the wisdom, and it must follow that, while some are
striving to gain that wisdom, some will, as a
matter of course, remain unquiet until they can
gain the religious graces which she alone bestows
with that wisdom. Walworth is one of these,
and, partly of his own accord and partly from
necessity, he crosses. There are others who will
have more difficulty in leaving friends and un-
doing a work which they had trusted was good.

"I am under many obligations to you for
Oakeley's letter and the *Lives of the Saints*, which
I return by McMaster.

"Please write to me and inform me how and
when I shall send you the Breviary and the *Lives
of the Saints* (Butler's) and also what I shall do
with the tools. I have lost the bill of the latter,
but if you wish to have them sold please say (if
you recollect) what they cost.

"Will it not be your pleasure to come and see
me this summer? I shall be here and at Wad-

hams Mills alternately. But will manage to have my time entirely at your disposal if I can receive so great a pleasure as your company. Please write to me soon, addressing me at this place.

"Very sincerely your friend,
"E. P. WADHAMS.

"Monday, May 19th.

"P. S. Agreeably to your request, I have destroyed my will this morning; and must beg of you to be set free of the trust committed to me in your own. Ever yours,
"E. P. WADHAMS."

The next letter which I give the reader is one from myself to Wadhams, detailing after some sort the circumstances which attended my reception into that great motherly bosom which I had sought for so earnestly, but had been so timid to recognize. The mail which bore it to Ticonderoga must have passed McMaster as he brought down to New York the letter just given above.

"IN FESTO CORPORIS CHRISTI, May, 1845.

"DEAR WADHAMS: You have not, of course, forgotten your poor crazy friend, who used to get so wild when you left him alone, and talked of *going over*. Well, he *has* gone over now, and his soul is as quiet and happy as if it had a right to be happy instead of mourning in sackcloth and ashes. For fear I should not have room afterwards, I will begin by telling you statistically and methodically what I have done. I arrived here

(New York) in due time on Wednesday morning, and the same day made my way to Father Rumpler. I found him all that I wished—a wise, kind, earnest, spiritually-minded man, and put myself immediately into his hands. Last Friday (May 16th) I made my profession—the form you have probably seen in the Roman Ritual. Three or four witnesses only were present, as I wished the matter to be secret, for tranquillity's sake, until I had received the sacraments. The creed of Pius IV. sounded most musically in my ears, and I took pleasure in repeating it very slowly and distinctly. I was then freed from the curse and excommunication which you remember used so to trouble us. On Thursday, the day before, I had made my confession, and on Saturday came again to the confessional and was absolved, and on Sunday morning communicated, after which I had no longer any motive to make the thing a secret. It is well known at the seminary, and, of course, therefore, in other quarters; but, as I have kept very much at home, I do not know what is said about it. None of those to whom I have spoken before my profession used the least expostulation, but seemed to regard it as a thing of course, and an honest step. McVickar is silent and reserved in the extreme, but very kind. I do not know what to infer from this, but am unwilling to trouble him. I have made application through Father Rumpler to be admitted as novice at Baltimore, and shall probably hear next week. I have as yet had no intercommunication with my immediate relatives in this matter. This, my severest trial, will come on next week. And now I have told you all that relates to myself externally. My inward joy and satisfaction at being in the very church of God and communion of the saints, I cannot express. Should Judge B—— express any interest in my movements, make no secret with him. I feel much attached to him, not only on account of his friendliness to me, but from strong personal esteem. Remember me gratefully to Mrs. B——, also to Clarence, and the other children. Alas! dear Wadhams, what shall I say to you, of your kindness, gentleness, and thousand favors to me? I will just say *nothing*, for I will not have my feelings belied by an attempt to convey them by letter.

"Well, what have you and Mac been doing in Essex County? Has he been raising any commotion in your extensive diocese? If he is with you still, give my warm love to him, although that is not very necessary, as I shall most probably be here when he comes down, and can do it for myself. I earnestly hope he will be cautious in the extreme in his method of abjuring his Protestant connections, for his own sake and that of others, and especially of the great cause. I do not mean he ought to do it precisely in the same still way as I—for, of course, every one must in some sort act according to his own natural method—but I mean he ought to say and do nothing without premeditation. So far as I have learned, Puseyism is still alive at the seminary, and wearing its own colors. It is scouring away at the outside of the cup and platter very bravely, as you remember it in our day there. The young Anglo-Catholics are acquiring the dyspepsia by fasting, buying up rosaries and crucifixes, which, nevertheless, they have no idea of using, and enjoy the satisfaction of knowing how frightened their mothers would be if they knew what their darlings were about. Perhaps this may seem to you somewhat *cross*, but indeed I am out of all conceit with Puseyism, whether ornamental, sentimental, or antiquarian. Christ is one and undivided, and must be sought for in His undivided church, which He inhabits and inspires. God grant that you and I may soon meet upon that Rock which rests itself upon the Rock of Ages!

"Give my sincere love to your mother—I shall not soon forget her, I assure you. Also to Mrs. Hammond and the doctor, Mrs. and Miss Hay, Mrs. Atherton, and all others who have been kind to me. If you will answer me *immediately*, I shall get your letter before I leave New York. With all my heart, most sincerely yours forever,

"CLARENCE WALWORTH.

"Direct to me at New York, care of Edgar Jenkins, Esquire, 78 Eleventh Street. I visit often the brethren of St. Alphonse, but will tell you more hereafter. C. W."

The words in the above letter which speak of our anxiety at the thought of living in a state of excommunication may require some explanation. To furnish this I give the following reminiscence: In Sterne's *Tristram Shandy* is a story, given there as a joke, but often repeated among Protestants as a reality. It represents that on Friday in Holy Week the Pope publicly curses all heretics and infidels from the altar. The curse is given word for word, and is really something very horrible. It is, in fact, just so near the truth as this: that on that day, in all Catholic churches throughout the world, public prayers are offered for their conversion, in order that God may bless them. We did not either of us give much credit to such a tale, but still we were ignorant in regard to the real facts. Wadhams, I remember, had been more struck by the awful nature of anathemas from such a source than moved to a feeling of resentment. "It's a foolish story," said he. "It can't be true. But, I tell you what!—I don't want that old man to curse me."

The next letter connects itself sufficiently with the preceding one, and is here given without comment:

"SARATOGA SPA, June 26th, 1845.

"DEAR WADHAMS: What can I write to you? I know you must be anxious to hear all the news; but, in such an ocean of things I have to tell you, what can one do with a sheet of paper? I wish

I had you here hung up fast by a hook in some corner where you could not get away. I would talk to you from sunrise to bed-time, and you would need to say nothing but 'no! no!—did?—did?' all the while. You will be surprised perhaps to find me writing from Saratoga. I came up about two weeks since, at mother's request and to try to comfort her, for she takes my conversion very much to heart, thinking me quite ruined by becoming a Catholic. I shall return in a very few days. By the by, the priest at the Springs is a *Cistercian*, or monk of St. Bernard (only think, a *genuine live Cistercian*), a very learned and, I think, a very good man. When Bishop Hughes travelled in Belgium this monk became much interested for this poor, infidelity-ridden country, and obtained leave to come and help the good cause on this side the water. You asked me in your last letter to describe to you the ways and customs of the brethren of St. Alphonse at New York. Indeed, I can tell you nothing beyond what M. has told you.

"In the first place, there are scarcely enough of them to constitute a 'house,' being only three, and sometimes four, Fathers, and a few lay-brethren. Then, again, I go in and out without ceremony and the Father Superior is almost always ready to see me, and as I am not put under rule, I know very little about their rule. McM., who stays with them all the while and is besides much more observing than I, is better able to

THE MONASTERY AT WADHAMS MILLS, N. Y.

inform you. But this will, of course, be entirely unnecessary, for you will soon come down to see us off—(of course, you have learned from Mac that we are to go to Europe—Belgium)—and make your profession before we go. Then you will see them all, and love them all as we do. We shall embark, probably, about the first of August with the Father Provincial from Belgium.

"Oh! what shall I say to you of the joys of Catholic communion, the frequent and the *real* Sacraments, the privilege of daily Mass, and constant access to a confidential director? How miserable do all the unrealities of Puseyite speculation appear to one who is a Catholic in fact and not in dreams! I cannot bear to think of you all alone among those godless hills, an exile from the church into which you were baptized, and conducting unauthorized conventicles. Do not, I beg of you for Christ's sake, delay making your profession long. At least discontinue your meetings. Forgive me for speaking so, my dearest friend and kind benefactor, but I speak earnestly, believing that nothing is so expedient for us as to do God's will promptly. I have had a letter from Platt, who 'thanks God' for my sake and says he told the bishop he did not blame me for escaping from the *torturing embrace* of the Episcopal Church, but he cannot yet make up his mind to follow my example. I have urged him to come to New York and see me before I go, and told him he would meet you there. I *presumed* you would not let us leave without seeing us, and Mac said he would urge you to come down. Indeed, you should make your profession and confession before Father Rumpler by all means, and you will gain much by coming and spending a while before, as we have already become familiar with the brethren and others. Although I have been in the habit of attending daily Mass, I doubt if I have forgotten you once in the presence of the Holy Victim. May the good Mother shield and bless you also, for I owe you very much, and, although I have always behaved more like a saucy companion, I assure you I look up to you as a father, not in years, but in care and kindness.

"Do not forget to remember me to your mother, whom I remember daily in my prayers; to Judge B——, also Clarence, and others whom I am bound to love. My eyes are constantly improving, yet I confess I feel the effects of this writing. Tell Mrs. Hammond, although our farm of St. Mary's is abandoned, in which she took such a kind interest, I hope she may live to bring many a rose and lily to the altar of our dear Lady. In the hope of giving you soon a right good Catholic embrace,

"Your affectionate friend and brother,

"CLARENCE 'ALBAN ALPHONSE.'

"The two names you see in my signature are the names by which I was confirmed. You will, of course, not use them as yet in directing letters."

The preceding two letters show that I had applied for admission into the Redemptorist Order and that I had been accepted by the Very Rev. Father De Held, Provincial, then on a visit to America, accompanied by Father Bernard, who afterwards succeeded to his office here. Father De Held was head of the Province of Belgium, which then included Holland, England, and the United States. These letters show also that I had been destined to make my novitiate, not at Baltimore, but at St. Trond, in Belgium. In the mean while McMaster had decided to join the same order, and so also had Isaac Hecker, now well known as first Superior of the Paulist Fathers of Fifty-ninth Street, New York City. The Provincial had decided not to keep us in waiting until his own return to Europe, but to send us on beforehand, and at once. Father Hecker was not one of our seminary set and had never been an Episcopalian. McMaster and I met him for the first time at the Redemptorist Convent in Third Street, after our reception there. He was himself only a year-old Catholic. He had had nothing to do with Puseyism, and knew very little about it. His chief experience lay in the New England school of Transcendentalism.

We little understood at first the full value that lay concealed under the long yellow locks that hung down over his broad shoulders and behind the bright eyes, which shone with an openness of enthusiasm which made us smile. On concluding to join us he had just sufficient time to hurry off to Baltimore, where Father De Held then was, get accepted, and hurry back again before the ship left port.

We considered it as contrary to holy poverty to go as first-class passengers; Hecker's brothers, however, took care to have a special room built up for all three in the second cabin. While these hurried preparations were in progress, the following letter was written:

"NEW YORK CITY, July 25th, 1845.

"DEAR WADHAMS: I intended to have given you earlier notice of the time of our departure, that you might have ample time to come and see us off at your leisure, but circumstances have turned up which oblige us to set off almost immediately, viz.: on Friday, the 1st of August. We shall cross in the London packet *Prince Albert*. I fear even now you will scarcely have time to come, there are so many chances of this letter being delayed. Most likely the packet will not get off until Saturday, the 2d, as I am told it is very common to delay a day or so, and sailors do not like to go out of port on a Friday. If I were going alone it would be great presumption to think you would come so far to see me, to whom you have no reason to be attached, except that you have shown me so much kindness and have given me so much reason to love you; but you and McMaster are older friends, and you will certainly wish to bid him 'farewell, and Godspeed,' before he sails. We shall both almost hold our breaths in expectation of you. It makes me very sad to think over our last winter's life. McM. tells me I am much in the habit of saying unpleasant things in a thoughtless way to my friends, and I doubt not it is true, although I was not aware of it before. How often I may have wounded your feelings last winter in this manner, for I know I talked very much and very thoughtlessly; but you, who were always so patient with me then, will not, I am sure, find it difficult to forget all these things now the time has gone by. As happy as I am to breathe the holy atmosphere of the Catholic Church, it is a bitter thing to leave my country—which I love all the more dearly for its pitiable religious destitution—and so many kind friends whom I may never see again in life. But it is very selfish to speak of myself now. Come down, dear Wadhams, at once, if you *possibly can*, and let me see your face again. We will talk over in one day more than a thousand letters can contain. What an age of awful responsibility we live in! How irresistible the impression that God has vast designs for the good of His church upon the very eve of accomplishment! Oh, what if He should call upon us at important and critical moments, and we should be found wanting! Let us cry out to God with groans and tears that we may be permitted to do and to *suffer* something in the good and holy cause. What have we to do with the enjoyment of the world, or even of the most tender family relations, which is all the same thing, while Christ is pleading with us: 'What, can ye not watch with me one hour?' It needs but a little time in the Roman Catholic Church to feel the depth and tenderness of her motherly love and care, and how blessed it is to labor in her cause, and to die in her arms. How can one 'fight the good fight and finish the faith' when joined to the abominations and covered with the trappings of heresy?

"How can one hope for the benediction of Jesus upon himself or his doings while he will not listen to the voice, 'Come, and follow Me'?

"Do come down at once and see us. Four years is a long time. Yesterday evening was the first we knew of the exact time of our departure, or I should have written before. God bless you, speed my letter, and bring you hither in time.

"Your faithful and grateful friend,
"CLARENCE WALWORTH.

"P. S.—I am living now all alone at my brother-in-law's, Mr. Jenkins, 78 Eleventh Street; but it would be more sure to come at once to McMaster's quarters in the house attached to the rear of the Catholic church on Third Street, between Avenues A and B."

The above letter was mailed to Ticonderoga, whence it was forwarded to Wadhams Mills. An indorsement on the back of the sheet of paper upon which it is written shows that Wadhams did not receive it until the day we sailed. Did not this fact add an additional pang to the reading of it? In any case it shows why he did not come to see us off.

Chapter IV.

Wadhams amid the Encircling Gloom. — "Lead Thou Me On."—Rostrums Against Romanism.—He Enters the Fold.

1845–1846.

WADHAMS was now almost entirely alone. His loneliness was not like that of Robinson Crusoe on his solitary island. He had neighbors around him. They knew him and loved him well, and were as much disposed to be sociable as ever. He was in the midst of family friends, and to a man like him these family ties were very dear. He would never lack for any sympathy which they could give him. But the kind of sympathy which he needed most they had not to give. They were Protestants, and all of them perfectly satisfied with that religion to which they were accustomed. His own mind, on the contrary, was filled with religious doubts, practical and pressing doubts, which called for a quick solution. His heart, therefore, was straitened by a deep anguish, the cause of which they could not understand. The kind of sympathy which they could give him was not that which could bring relief. Those to whom he had been accustomed to open his heart, because they stood on the same ground with him and could understand him, were now gone. The broad Atlantic lay between him and them. They were happy and he was not. They could have sympathized with him and shown their sympathy if they had remained with him, but they were gone. They had gone forward and so left him. Others had recoiled backward and anchored their hearts behind him. He was thus quite alone, with none to share his anguish. Where was there a sympathizing heart to whom he could open his own?

Of course, there is one Friend above all others, and by that Friend the just man is never forsaken. Sympathy with Him is never broken by any circumstances; but only converts who have passed through the deep waters in which Wadhams was now struggling know how clouds of darkness gather about the soul at times, and make it participate in some measure in that desolation which caused the Lord-Christ on His cross to cry out: "My God, my God, why hast Thou forsaken me?" I know of one who once, in a moment of desolation of this kind, which came in the middle of the night, could only find relief by rising from his bed, and on his bare knees protesting that, if God would only show him what to do, he would do it, let the cost be what it might. "Surely," he said, "God cannot damn me while I say this, and mean it." Those who have passed through similar trials are best able to understand the deep meaning which lies in those words of Cardinal Newman, now so familiar to the public:

"Lead, kindly light, amid the encircling gloom
Lead thou me on."

Of course in these cases, when a young churchman is thought to be in danger of going over to Rome, friends are not wanting who are ready to offer sympathy, such as it is, and there are spiritual doctors among them to prescribe infallible remedies. These remedies generally consist in urging the patient to do precisely what his conscience will not let him do. They succeed in curing only those whose consciences are not thoroughly aroused, or who are weak in the knees. These various remedies are in substance reducible to three or four—such, for instance, as: "Take advice," "Take orders," "Take a parish," "Take a wife."

The first letter from Wadhams' correspondence which belongs to this period of spiritual desolation, covering something less than a year, is from a seminarian of his own class, the Rev. Edwin A. Nichols. It dates from "New York, June 2d, 1845;" and contains prescriptions for Wadhams' spiritual malady, beginning with the first in the order given above—namely, to *take advice*. After a brief introduction, he says:

"I proceed *in medias res*, and perhaps you anticipate what is coming. We have not been much surprised to hear that McMaster has joined the Roman Catholic community in this country; but Mr. Walworth's move has rather taken *me* aback, although I knew little of him personally. Of course we are ready to conclude that you and he consulted on this matter together before he left you, and I suppose you will not be surprised if your old friends ask, 'Will Wadhams go next?' Now, will you allow me the privilege of an old friend, to take you (as it were) by the hand and say to you, 'Think before you leap'? I well recollect one of McMaster's rash expressions, that he was going 'to take a leap in the dark.' However, I believe you would not do that. . . . We were ordained together: I should be sorry to think you have ever found any grounds for doubting the validity of that ordination. If Carey, with all his great learning and devoted piety, believed those orders valid, it should counterbalance the weight of a good many Walworths, etc., the other way. Besides, it is no news to you that their validity has been admitted by many Roman Catholics themselves. *Courayer* you have perhaps read, also Bishop England of Charleston, a prominent Roman Catholic divine lately deceased. However, it seems to me hardly possible that your mind has been altered on this point, and that all the treasures of ancient and modern English theology, with which your commonplace books are stored, have become to you so much dross. Here then, I hope, you will act differently from Walworth. He (I understand) took the advice of none of our learned divines, but went 'on his own hook,' adopting the sectarian plan of neglecting reason and argument, and seeking from *prayer alone* that guidance which sober piety would hardly expect without faithfully using *all the means* which Providence has placed within our reach. . . . Supposing, then, that you may have been troubled with doubts, would it not be your duty to consult with some of your respected brethren and fathers in the church before allowing your mind to become *changed*, or even *unsettled*, with regard to any of the church's doctrines or principles? Doubtless you will agree with me on this point. Allow me, then, to hope that you will not suffer your mind to be imperceptibly warped and weaned from the church of your *first* love until you have had *free and full intercourse* with some of our clergy whom you know and respect as 'pillars in the church of Christ.' "

The above citation of Courayer and Bishop England for the validity of English orders is rather unfortunate. Courayer was an apostate Catholic. He first embraced Jansenism and afterwards Anglicanism. It will be news to Catholics that Bishop England made any such admission. Moreover, the fact is well known that, when Anglicans in orders become Catholics, they have to be reordained. This practice rests upon a very early decision made at Rome in the case of a converted English clergyman. It was certain that Wadhams' own mind was so far unsettled in this matter at the time of receiving this letter that he had no confidence in his own ordination as deacon, and persistently refused to go on and take priest's orders.

To urge either Wadhams or myself, or McMaster, McVickar, Whicher, Platt, Donelly, or many others who might be named in the same category, to take advice from living "pillars" of the Episcopal Church was simply nonsense. What had we been doing during our seminary course but studying the very questions on which we were asked to seek light? The necessity of ordination to constitute a priest, the apostolical succession, and the validity of Anglican orders, the nature and characteristic notes of a true church, the essential doctrines and sacraments necessary to constitute and furnish the true Christian church—these were the very subjects which we had studied most anxiously, in class and out of class, with the aid of all the eminent "pillars" which Anglicanism could afford. The longer we studied, and the deeper our application to these questions, the more we felt the want of foundation beneath our feet; and what other foundation could these wonderful "pillars" have, and why should we risk our salvation on their *dictamina?* Among Anglican clergymen there were not a few that we knew well and respected much as gentlemen, as scholars, and as sincere Christians;

but how could they be "pillars of the church" to us, or add anything to our security? To take advice of such as they in our position did not mean humility, nor docility, nor that prudence which comes from heaven. It meant to dose our consciences with morphine, committing ourselves to men who were already committed. It could only mean, in our case, a cowardly surrender of conscience, with a hypocritical expedient to back up the surrender. I am willing and glad to admit that there are some rare men who know how to give advice with a regard solely to the state of an honest conscience which seeks it. Dr. Alonzo Potter, formerly bishop of Pennsylvania, was a man of this kind. An acquaintance and friend of mine was once a clergyman in his diocese and with a conscience struggling and hesitating like that of Wadhams. In a moment of feebleness he went to his bishop, opened his mind to him, and put himself under his direction, not doubting what that direction would be. He was astonished at the answer he got. "If," said the bishop, "the state of your mind is such as you represent, I am sorry for it; but there is only one course conscientiously open to you. It is to join the Roman Catholic Church. In any case," he added, "I can no longer consent to your officiating in my diocese." Such advice is very rare, but such men as Dr. Potter are also very rare. It is scarcely necessary to say that the young cleric in question took this advice immediately.

He has been for these many long years a most talented and estimable priest in the Catholic Church.

I had occasion once to give a very different advice. A Methodist minister, whose name I did not ask, once came to me at St. Mary's, representing that he had strong inclinations to become a Catholic and a priest. He had many questions to ask, but his questions were not of a character to do him much credit. His chief anxiety was to know what salary a priest could command, and what other means he had to make his way through the world. I told him that nothing less than a bishop could attend to a case like his. He asked if I would recommend him to apply to the bishop. I said: "You may go to him if you like, but if you should you will probably find that I have been there before you, and advised him to have nothing to do with you." This was not a case of uneasy conscience, but of dilapidated finance. Any of the usual prescriptions administered to perplexed converts would have suited his case—orders, or a parish, or a wife, or any other profitable advice.

Nichols was not satisfied in his letter with urging Wadhams to take advice. He had another remedy in reserve, which was to keep him as busily employed as possible in the church where he found himself. This, with a glowing description of his own work, and the happiness he found in it, occupies nearly all the rest of the letter. Nichols was pastor of the "Emmanuel Church" in New York. His location and special relations with McVickar and others appear from the following passage:

"Our members have increased in number, and apparently in zeal also. Our singing is very spirited and good. Sunday-school is somewhat the worse from want of efficient teachers. H. McVickar has been teaching a class through the winter, but has recently left, as he is about going out of town for the season. More than this, we have concluded the bargain for the purchase of a church, and where do you think it is? Corner of Prince and Thompson Streets—in other words, the one in which Dr. Seabury now officiates, a place well known to us both of old. The Annunciation people are going to build a new church up-town, and in the mean while are to go in the chapel of the university, and then we take possession of their church building as a Free Church."

Wadhams' correspondence during the winter of 1845 and 1846 contains three letters from his friend McVickar, the greater part of which would not be very interesting to the reader. They show him still remaining at Columbia College without having taken orders. Although he had abandoned his project of engaging in a monastic life with Wadhams in Essex County, he continued to interchange books with him and matters of intelligence, especially matters regarding the

Oxford movement, both in England and America. They show a constant diminution of his own active interest in that movement. In one he says: "Experience teaches me that to trust in myself or any man is to lean upon a broken reed. Therefore, look up to Dr. Pusey or any other man as a leader, I will not."

In a letter dated January 30th he intimates a certain shifting of the scenery in the Puseyism of New York which is not without interest. After detailing several novelties of practice and worship introduced in New York and Brooklyn, he instances St. Luke's Church in Hudson Street, of whose rector he says: "I think I told you Mr. Forbes has early communion every Sunday except the second in the month, and recommends and hears confessions. He is gaining the influence which Dr. Seabury is losing at the seminary."

With the fading of that hope which once led him on, the hope of engrafting something higher and better on the dead branches of Anglicanism, comes the necessity of doing something else. Either one must go forward to Rome or settle down to rest where one is. But, for a true man, there is no rest without work. McVickar's letters show that he now began to feel it necessary to take orders, and find for himself occupation in the Anglican ministry. At the same time he shows a great desire to engage Wadhams to enter into some new and larger field of ministerial labor which might serve to tranquillize him. He suggests that Dr. Whittingham, bishop of Maryland, was in search of clergymen. He writes: "Bishop McCoskey, I understand, says he could fill twenty stations if he had the men." He then adds: "Bishop Ives has just called here. I mentioned your name to him. He is in want, he says, of some clergy of clear Catholic views and practice, to assist in establishing the tone of his diocese. Do you know him? I am sure you would like him."

The reader will readily recognize the name last mentioned. Dr. Ives was then bishop of North Carolina; he afterwards became a convert to the ancient church, in which he lived as a layman. He is well known to Catholics as the founder of the Catholic Protectory near New York City, and other charitable enterprises. His wife was a daughter of the famous John Henry Hobart, Protestant bishop of New York. She followed her husband into the church. McVickar was shortly afterwards ordained an Episcopalian deacon, and died of consumption in a few months.

Several other letters are found among Wadhams' papers, written by his former fellow-seminarians, which belong to this same period of anxious doubt and hesitation. One of these is from Mr. Bostwick, a clergyman settled at Brandon, Vt. He belonged to the same circle of seminarians with Carey and others, and his name is found mentioned more than once in Wadhams' correspondence. His career in matters of religion no longer ran parallel with that of our friend, for he had taken to himself a wife. Children had begun to grow around his hearth. These needed providing for, and his parishioners of Brandon owed back salary to their last pastor, and under these embarrassing circumstances they judged it to be imprudent to pay their present pastor any at all. The Vermont hills afforded "a fine prospect, but poor eating." The letter contains other things of a more spiritual character, but no attempt is made to advise Wadhams or administer interior comfort.

Among the letters belonging to this period and preserved by Wadhams is one of peculiar interest. This interest is derived not merely from the fact that the writer was a fellow-seminarian, and deeply involved in the new Oxford movement, but because in it he delineates so fully and clearly his own position of doubt, anxiety, and distress, and gives also the motives which drew him towards the Catholic Church and those which held him back. His position was very much the same as that of Wadhams, although, unlike Wadhams, he did not become a Catholic. We omit the writer's name, because he is still living, and may have the same or similar prudential reasons for reticence which, as he himself intimates, existed at the time of writing. The letter is dated March 3d, 1846. After some preliminary excuses for not writing sooner, it says:

"How great—how very great changes have taken place since we met! how many friends have gone from us! how many among us have shrunk back! I must confess that when the 'secession' first took place, I felt very miserable, very desolate and unhappy; and still at times I find myself giving way to such feelings, but I have become, as a general thing, more reconciled to it; and, believing as I do most firmly that God is with us still as a part of His holy church, and that there are holy men among us to act as His instruments, I am becoming more warmly attached to our holy, afflicted mother, and will pray and strive that she may be lifted out of the dust. She cannot now be invited to the centre of Catholic unity, but the time for that union *will* come, and it seems to me my duty to labor *in* and *for* her that she may be prepared for it. I do think that changes in matters of practice, and in some matters of requirement, must take place in the Mother Church before the daughter can become reconciled to her, and God, who is all powerful, will bring about those changes in His good time, and will bring about that union, too, for which we so much long.

"But here I am writing on without being mindful, dear Wadhams, that you differ with me on some of these points. We may see things alike yet; and whichever of us may be wrong I pray God to lead to the truth. I have gotten over that dread, even for the truth itself, which I once felt,

Rev. Clarence A. Walworth, LL.D.

and am ready and anxious to receive it now *wherever* and *whatever* it may be.

"Only, dear brother, if you *can conscientiously* stand by our church in this her day of sorrow, do not forsake her; believe me, though you are isolated in position, yet there are more hearts than you think beating in sympathy with yours.

"I see Mr. Hoyt has resigned his parish. Do you know what he is going to do? Tell me all you know about Bostwick; I have not heard from him for a long time. . . ."

The Rev. Mr. Hoyt mentioned in the above letter was a married clergyman of St. Albans, Vt., who soon after the above writing, and about the same time as Wadhams, entered the Catholic Church with all his family. After the death of his wife, he took priest's orders. At his first Mass eight of his children received communion from his hands. One of his daughters is now a contemplative nun of the Dominican Order and of the strictest observance. Another became a nun of the Sacred Heart, and died a most holy death in that order. Many other kinsmen of this family have become Catholics. The recent death of Father Hoyt, although, of course, on many accounts an affliction to his friends, occurred under circumstances which lent a peculiar beauty to the event. The death-stroke fell upon him while celebrating Mass, and immediately after his communion. In this way, by the providence of God, he received his Viaticum at the altar and administered by himself. He neither spoke nor tasted anything after this. His last words were the words of the Mass, and his last food was Food from heaven.

I am glad to find among the letters written to Wadhams at this period some from the Rev. Charles Platt. He was a first cousin of mine, and had an intimate acquaintance with Wadhams, dating from their seminary life together. He was a man of high scholarship and fine talents, and a clear, sound judgment, with a most innocent and excellent boyhood behind him, like Wadhams' own. I cannot venture to omit his letters altogether, because they represent so graphically the spirit of the Oxford movement in America, with all that young life which filled the bosoms of our seminarians and fresh graduates from the seminary. How near Platt was to the Catholic Church may be learned from the opening sentence of a letter which he sent to me near the close of July, 1845, just before my departure for Europe. It was in answer to one of mine informing him of my conversion, announcing my departure, and asking him to come to New York and see me off. It ran thus:

"DEAR COUSIN: I thank my God that your feet are at last planted upon the 'Rock of Peter.' I cannot, however, close with your invitation to come to New York and see you embark. To accept that invitation would mean that I am ready to become a Catholic, and I am not. I cannot break my mother's heart. . . ."

A letter from Whicher at the same time, and in answer to a similar invitation, announced to me that he had decided to come, but had changed his mind on learning that Platt would not. Platt died out of the Fold many years later, leaving a wife and children. Whicher also married, and twice, taking parishes at Clayville and Whitesboro' in Oneida County. It was ten years before he took the great step. After that he was living in Oneida County, a Catholic layman. His first wife is known to literature as the "Widow Bedott." The second became a Catholic shortly after himself. Platt's first letter to Wadhams runs as follows:

"ROCHESTER, Dec. 31st, 1845.

"MY DEAR FRIEND: It was not my intention to follow your example of delay, but circumstances have placed my time out of my own control. I have lately understood from Clarence's friends that he had arrived at Belgium. His Protestant connections cannot, of course, see any reason for his course, and set it down as a vagary from which he will eventually return. Sometimes, in view of the quiet and communion with the sainted which he must now strongly experience, I have been tempted to the wish, 'Oh, that I had the wings of a dove!' but such thirstings are only the signs of a struggle, and not really the best relief for us. Poor Pollard! He never crossed my sight; yet I cannot help feeling drawn toward him in the hour of his oppression—an oppression the more hateful under a system which provides no remedy. If the mere breathing of Catholic truth is thus to be choked out of one, woe worth the day! However, let them rue it that need; it is not the sufferer's part. . . .

"And now I beg you not to be so dilatory again, nor to complain of my remissness. I hear nothing directly from Clarence or 'Mac.' Believe me, yours in bonds,

"C. H. PLATT."

The news from Europe which Platt could not furnish came directly to Wadhams in a letter from me, dated at St. Trond, Belgium, February 7th, 1846. It reads:

"DEAR WADHAMS: You are no doubt surprised that I have not written to you long ago. I assure you it is a matter which has disturbed me not a little. It is a debt I owe you, not only of friendship, but of gratitude, and I have been very uneasy at my inability to discharge it. But the necessary duties of each day have been a severe tax upon my eyes, and I had much writing to do which it was impossible to neglect, so that I have been debarred from letter-writing. Hitherto I have written only three letters to America—two of them to my parents, and one to Preston."

I remember this letter to Preston (the late Mgr. T. S. Preston, Vicar-General of the Archdiocese of New York), then a Protestant seminarian at Twentieth Street. John Henry Newman had at last passed through the "encircling gloom," and closed his sharp, short struggle with pain by openly and fully professing the Catholic faith and joining the true Fold. In adverting to this event, the news of which had just reached our convent, I spoke of Dr. Pusey's comment upon it. It is stated that he said, with an air of quiet resignation: "Well, it is all right; the Roman Catholics have prayed harder than we, and so they have got him!" When this was told to Father Othmann, our novice-master, he was disgusted, and said: "This language is neither rational nor manly. It is nothing but baby talk." I repeated this in my letter to Preston, who replied indignantly that he did not agree with me at all; that Dr. Pusey's sentiment was that of a man both reasonable and spiritual. There must have been hard praying on our side for Preston in New York, for not very long after this the Catholics scored a similar victory in his case. But to return to my letter to Wadhams:

"I have just been allowed a dispensation from all the common exercises of the novitiate except the daily conference, in order to open my heart a little to some of my far-off friends in America, and I begin with you. You cannot conceive how much I want you here. I do not know how to excuse myself for not having brought you away forcibly upon my back. Ah! if the *quondam abbot* of Wadhams Mills were only here, where the discipline of the religious life is found in all its wisdom, vigor, and attractiveness, he would weep and laugh by turns with me at our futile 'monkery' among the hills of Essex. He would believe readily what Father Rumpler told me at New York, that the Puseyites have found only the *carcass* of Catholicism, while the soul, the life, the breath of God, the spirit of holiness is hidden from them. You remember our many conversations of last winter, how we lamented the want of religious system, and of guidance for the conscience, and how we magnified the happiness of Catholics and especially the religious who live under direction. I can answer for it we were both sincere and earnest. But for myself I confess I scarcely knew what I talked about. Judge B—— thought us not a little romantic. I wish he might see the reality. Romance would seem tame. I deny that I had any romantic thoughts when I came here; but, if I had, a few months' routine would dissipate that. To get up at half-past four every morning at the sound of bell, precisely, neither before nor after; to go to bed at half-past nine of necessity, and all day long in the mean time to sit or stand or move at the sound of the convent clock, the remorseless clock which makes no account of the particular inspirations you may have at the moment; to make recreation with the others whether you *feel like it or not*, in short, to have your own way in *nothing*—this may be romance to Puseyites, who eat and sleep and pray at their leisure, but here at St. Trond it is a sober, every-day sort of business. No, there is no romance about it. For a man who is not in earnest to save his soul, who has neither the fear of hell, the love of God, nor the desire of holiness, it is dull play. But for one who is disgusted with his sins, and mourns the hardness of heart and sensuality which separates him from God, who loves the character of Jesus Christ, and burns with desire to imitate it, this Congregation of St. Alphonsus Liguori is a 'treasure-trove,' to which he will cling as a drowning man clings to whatever will support him. I assure you I had no conception of the real value of spiritual direction, and especially such direction as is found in the novitiate. Here there is no guile, none of those constant little deceptions which even the most honest in the world abound with. The whole heart is opened to your superior. Prepared by the experience of years, he scrutinizes your character and temperament, and explains to you your characteristic faults, and the means by which you must seek to do away with them. He watches your daily progress and teaches you to know yourself and watch yourself. Here we find rigor, but the rigor is in the rule and not in the manner. Love is the presiding spirit, and even the rule must bend to charity. We are a perfect family—fathers, children, brothers. We know each other well, and understand mutually the different peculiarities of character, and thus distrust is altogether banished, while the common life, the common interest, the common hopes, the congregation which links us all together inseparably until we shall be called to join the more perfect congregation of heaven make harmony and mutual love unavoidable. Here, my dear friend, is a home for you. I cannot doubt that you have a vocation to such a life. Your past history, so much as I know of it, your tastes and preferences, and the desire you have so long had for a monastic life are proof of it. It is a missionary order also, and in it better than anywhere else you can discharge your duty to God and your country. Believe me, the Redemptorists will raise a commotion yet in Essex County. The sincere love I bear you, as well as the desire I have that you and McMaster and I, with many others such as you, native Americans and still Protestants, may go up together in the cause of Christ against the devils which pervert the hearts of the American people, and hinder their salvation, stimulate me to write you in this manner. I know the difficulties in your way; but they are of the flesh—human. They are opportunities which God affords you of beginning with a sacrifice as an earnest of your fidelity. Certainly, how can one hope to gain heaven by the way of the cross when he is cowed by the first difficulty which presents itself? I also had my difficulty of the same nature. I will not concede that I love my mother less than you love yours. But now I am sure that, by becoming a Catholic, I have created strong reasons for my parents and others to think more tenderly of Catholics and Catholicism than before. But, after all, this is not the great question—it is enough that the voice of God calls all men to His Church, and declares that he who is not with Him is against Him. The sects of this day in controversy with that Church, as well as the ancient sects, were not created by God to gather in His elect; and how can one *who knows the Catholic Church* seek for salvation in them? Forgive me all this, dear Wadhams; it is on my heart and I must needs out with it. I cannot rest content when I think how one noble resolution would carry you to New York to make your profession and then hither to this *heaven on earth*, for of your vocation I cannot doubt. Do not, I beseech you, counsel with those whom you know to be sunk in heresy up to the hair, or guided by mere worldly motives, or, like H——, paralyzed by timidity. I desired to enclose a little *billet* in the letter McMaster wrote you, but he sent it off without thinking of me. He desires to be kindly remembered to you. He sets to work now to humble himself in the spirit of obedience with the same zeal as when a Puseyite he thought to erect dioceses and create bishops. You would scarcely know him. The Catholic Church has a gentle hand, but a nervous one.

"Indeed, now that I am living under her direct influence, there has grown up a feeling of her mysterious power which is far more forcible than the arguments which convinced me before. I have a great deal that I want to say to you, but in so short a compass what can I do? I would like to give you some description of our life here, which I know would so much interest you. I wrote Preston a minute account of our daily exercises; but you cannot see that, as you are so far away from New York. But I will give you some idea in brief: We have here twelve Fathers, or missionaries, who are about half the time on missions, and half in convent; some fifteen lay-brothers; besides these our "Père Maître" of novices, and his associate the "Père Socius," with twenty novices. We rise at half-past four, breakfast at half-past seven, dine at twelve, sup at seven, and go to bed at half-past nine. We have an hour's recreation together after dinner and another after supper, when we may converse together. All the rest of the day is spent in silence. Friday and Thursday are excepted, the first a day of constant silence and retreat, the latter one of general recreation. We have nearly two hours' time each day to spend in bodily exercise and manual labor. All the rest of the day is occupied either in private prayer and spiritual reading or in the various public exercises of the novitiate. The perfect regularity of everything about the convent would make you wonder. All is obedience, and obedience makes order easy. No time is wasted. The whole day is occupied. But I can give you no idea of our life here. It is so entirely different from everything you find in the world. It would require a book to describe it. A full insight into a convent would be in itself an all-sufficient refutation of Protestantism. It would show also how utterly impossible was our scheme to establish the conventual life out of the Church, because out of the Church no one can be found to whom monastic obedience is due. A number of persons may *agree to obey* Breck or some other Protestant, but such obedience cannot be perfect nor last long. The authority of the superior must come from God through the sanction of His Church. The mere agreement of men cannot create it. This Puseyite idea is in itself a thoroughly Protestant notion. For my part I would shudder to submit the welfare of my body and soul to any other authority than that of God, and that authority we Catholic religious find in our superiors. But I have made already a very long letter, and must close. God knows how I long to see you, and see you safely delivered from your perilous position. You have created by your past kindness an obligation to love you, and I never forget you, nor your excellent mother, at the Holy Sacrifice.

Please write me, or better yet, come yourself, and let us tread together this dangerous road of life, and seek under the same rules and the same guidance to wash white our garments and prepare to meet Our Lord at His coming. Give my love to your kind mother, and my remembrance to Mrs. Hammond and family, Judge B—— and family. God and our dear Lady defend and guide you. Your faithful friend ever,

"CLARENCE WALWORTH.

"P. S.—I cannot think of leaving so large a space unfilled when we have so little opportunity of communication. I might tell you of our voyage across the ocean to Portsmouth, of Winchester Cathedral (of which however, we saw the outside only from the cars), of London, Westminster Abbey, the tomb of St. Edward the Confessor within it, etc. Splendid old Abbey! it made me melancholy to see it, like an old giant bound and helpless in a godless city. It presents a long history; almost from the time of the Conquest. Constant additions of chapels were made to it until the Reformation—and since then constant decay. Here and there you see headless figures, broken by Cromwell's soldiers and others, but no repairs. The Protestants now do not know what to do with it. They use a large transept to bury play-actors and poets, and have set apart a kind of meeting-house in the middle of it which looks like a little Protestant pill which the noble old abbey has been constrained to swallow, but the greater part has been unused and therefore is the less abused. The Church of St. Saviour, by the London Bridge, is also very ancient, and pleased McMaster better than the abbey; but it is unfortunately occupied. If I were with you I should have a great deal to say of what we have seen and heard, but as it is I can do nothing. There are churches not far from us which we have visited sometimes Thursdays, when on promenade, which would make your heart rejoice could you see them. I have thought of you more than once when looking at them, because you enjoy such things more than I. For my part I like better the architecture and ornaments of my little square cell; the table and crucifix hanging over it; the wooden cross lying on my bed, my bedfellow at night; the three-cornered black hat hanging over the door, my companion in the promenades; a little many-tailed cord with which on Wednesdays and Fridays we warm ourselves before going to bed; the black habit which covers me, and the Rosary at my belt, please my simple Anglo-Saxon taste. They remind me of my resemblance in the outward circumstances to so many glorious saints, cloister saints, while they cover me with confusion, to think that this resemblance is all on the outside. But this is too much like twaddle. I have but *one idea* when I think of you. I beg of you, my dear friend, in the name of Our Saviour, who made Himself homeless and a wanderer in the world for our sake, to surrender at once to your conscience, and declare yourself openly on His side. What advantage is it to read every day the lives of the saints, and their self-sacrifices, and still remain, through human respect, natural affection, or the dread of a transitory suffering of mind in a church which has no more solidity of faith or practice than a bag of wind is solid? Forgive me if I am too rude. I do not mean to be so. You know well that in my heart I have no other sentiments towards you than love and esteem. Farewell! May God bless you! Do not neglect the Holy Mother of God, who will not fail to help you if you pray to her. She is a better friend and counsellor than you will find in the Protestant Episcopal Church of the United States and England, which Newman, Oakeley, Faber, and others have left. Where do you find your *fellows* now? Nowhere, dear Wadhams, unless you consent to fall back on those behind you, and if you commence to fall back where will you stop? If you wish to learn anything of our order or receive guidance for the conscience from one who knows how to guide tenderly and well, consult Father Rumpler at New York, either by visit or by letter. (Rev. Gabriel Rumpler, C.SS.R., Third Street, New York.)"

The time had now come when Wadhams took his first positive step with reference to a possible union with the Roman Catholic Church. He held an official position in the Protestant Episcopal Church, and was in charge of a missionary field of labor therein. This fixed upon him a certain responsibility toward that church. It gave him certain duties in it, and so far abridged his independence. In case of deciding to become a Catholic he was not free to step from one church into the other without a show, at least, of inconsistent conduct. For instance, to become a Catholic on Thursday would make it difficult to preach in a Protestant pulpit on the Sunday before, or administer the rites of worship there. The doctrine and the worship which would be suitable to his conscience on Thursday would look like treachery in a Protestant church on Sunday. The fact that unfavorable comments are actually made in such cases shows that there are rules of honesty and propriety to be observed by converts, which are nevertheless embarrassing, and which require caution and deliberation. Wadhams was both honest and wise; and, therefore, to make himself independent, he began by resigning his charge in time. A second letter, which we now give, from the Rev. Charles Platt, alludes to this resignation of Wadhams' mission in Essex County:

"ST. PAUL'S, ROCHESTER, West N. Y.

"Monday in Holy Week, April 6th, 1846.

"MY DEAR WADHAMS: I hasten to answer yours of the 27th ult. After hope long deferred, you have truly relieved me. I had grown quite anxious about you, not knowing but your health had failed, or you had lost confidence in my sympathy with you, or you had already taken a step which would, indeed, sever us widely. I am glad to learn that you are yet holding fast to your contentment as well as your confidence, but I must regret that any circumstances should have forced you to cease from your labors for good. Forced you must have been, for no ruggedness of the field would deter you, nor any common hardships have driven you from your work.

"From your letter I hardly know what to make of your intentions. You seem to have relinquished your connection with the missionary operations of our church. Do you mean by that to say that you disconnect yourself from any ministerial labor in the church? I rather surmised that you were inclined to follow Clarence and McMaster. If so, we are outwardly severed—probably in your opinion altogether severed. I do not doubt that they were both acting with a good conscience—perhaps with a clearer conscience than I shall ever know. But I cannot in conscience follow them. Mr. Newman's *Essay* I have not read. I began it but had not time during Lent to finish it deliberately. . . .

"Whicher is in priest's orders. He had a hard time winter before the last. They passed him to the priesthood last fall; but he was plump with them, and kept nothing back. . . .

"I am surprised that you should leave your parish before Easter. This is the season, if any, to labor in our church, and to humble the Protestant pride. I have heard nothing from Clarence directly. Should like to hear very much.

"Yours,
"C. H. PLATT."

This is the last letter in my possession received by Wadhams while yet a Protestant. In less than three months he had passed beyond those days of doubt and desolation. He communicated the joyful intelligence to me in a letter which found me in Belgium, still in my novitiate, and preparing to make my vows. I am sorry not to have preserved it. It would be a treasure now.

It is strange that when the long agony was at an end, and Wadhams' resolution was taken to "cross over," the crossing was not found to be easy. A priest was necessary to receive him. And who should be that priest? Naturally the nearest priest would answer the purpose. Why not go to him? This is just what he did, although that priest was a perfect stranger to him. It is said that he entered a Catholic church or chapel in his own native Adirondacks, but after a brief conference with the priest he was allowed to depart without encouragement. As Wadhams turned away the clergyman said to one of his parishioners: "Look after that young man; I wonder what he is up to!"

His second attempt was made at Albany. He rang the bell at the door of St. Mary's rectory, then a bishop's residence. He made known his state of mind and wishes to an ecclesiastic of the house, and was answered, so it is said: "We are very busy here, and can't attend to you." Wonderful that this should have occurred àt the very door through which he so often afterward passed on holy errands of duty and charity when himself officiating there as a Catholic priest. His third and more successful application was made to the Sulpicians of St. Mary's Seminary, Baltimore. Here the future Bishop of Ogdensburg was cordially received, duly prepared, and admitted to that great Motherly Bosom so patiently sought for, so lovingly clung to.

Chapter V.

Wadhams' Life at the Sulpician Seminary, Baltimore.

1846–1850.

THE life of Edgar P. Wadhams now enters upon a new epoch. He dwells beneath a new sky. He breathes a new air. All his surroundings are new. His old companions are all still dear to him, but in one sense they are far away. They no longer see by the same light; they no longer look at the same stars. Their religious intercourse is broken up; and yet, to a true Christian, that intercourse of soul with soul is the best, holiest, sweetest that life affords. It follows, therefore, very naturally that almost all of Wadhams' correspondence changes. The familiar friends of earlier days for the most part cease to write letters, or at least such letters as men love to lay by for re-perusal. I find among Wadhams' papers a letter from the Rev. Armand Charbonnel, dated August 6th, 1846. Before he entered the seminary at Baltimore, Wadhams must have visited Vermont, where he made or renewed an acquaintance with Father Charbonnel. This French priest was a Sulpician, had been a professor at St. Mary's Seminary,

Baltimore, and afterwards at St. Sulpice, Montreal, and still later became Bishop of Toronto. He had advised him to prepare for the priesthood by entering the seminary at Montreal, or still better, if possible, to make his studies at Rome or Paris.

In his letter Father Charbonnel communicates to Wadhams the conversion of Rev. Mr. Hoyt, already referred to. This connects naturally with the current of our reminiscences and is a matter of interest. We give it in the words of the letter:

"Rev. Mr. Hoyt, of St. Albans, made his First Communion on last Sunday week, after having been previously baptized and absolved; and he received again on last Sunday, when his wife and four children were baptized and confirmed, as well as himself. He is a man of learning and property, but not settled as yet about what he will do. His countenance is remarkably sweet and noble; as for his lordship, Bishop Hopkins, he is mad with our new brother's change, or perversion. *Requiescat in pace.* He went so far lately, speaking against Catholics on that occasion, that one of his near relatives, a Protestant, left the church crying out: 'I am sick with such a bitterness!'"

It will be remembered that this Bishop Hopkins of Vermont had a public controversy with Archbishop Kenrick of Baltimore, in which the principal question discussed was the validity of Anglican orders. I recall to mind that Arthur Carey had at one time lived in Vermont in familiar relations with Bishop Hopkins, either as an inmate of his household or pupil in one of his schools, and always spoke of him as a man of great intelligence and learning.

I fear the reader is already wearied with so many letters. The narrative of events, personal recollections, and anecdotes are livelier and easier reading. But to historical minds that value faithful reality more, who wish to see the past just as it existed to the eyes of those who lived in the past, letters have a deeper interest. However, be this as it may, letters henceforth will not figure much in these reminiscences. We give just one more. It is a voice from across the sea, addressed to the abbot of St. Mary's, now dethroned, and a student at the seminary in Baltimore. It is a joyous and affectionate hail from the disbanded community of one.

"WITTEM, December 1st, 1846.

"MY DEAR WADHAMS: You see I date from another place, because, having happily finished my novitiate at St. Trond, and taken the vows, I am now busy like yourself in preparing for the priesthood. You have some idea perhaps of the great joy I felt on receiving your letter and finding you safely anchored in the harbor of the Church. God be thanked, my dear friend, that we have no longer to deal with the shuffling principles of Puseyism, but with the firm, unchanging, and unshaken faith! I should have written you a reply long ago to testify my joy at the happy step you have taken, but thought I would delay until I had made my vows; and the new circumstances in which I find myself have occasioned still further delay, for I am scarcely yet domesticated in my new abode. The liberty I took to chatter to you about your vocation was wholly on the supposition of your being at Wadhams Mills all alone among Protestants. Of course, you have now spiritual guides and every means of determining to what life God calls you. May our Blessed Lord grant you a long and useful life and the souls of many of your countrymen to testify in your favor at the day of judgment. I would love still to embrace you as a Redemptorist, but that is a matter with which I ought not to meddle too much. I will commend your vocation to our Blessed Lady, who knows what is best for you and for the good cause. McMaster, you know of course, has left us. He carries our good wishes and prayers with him. He made a long and careful trial of his vocation, and though it was found that God did not call him to the religious state, still, his good will will find its reward. His departure was much regretted by all his fellow-novices, who loved him and speak always of him with much affection. Of course, you can conceive the feelings of us two Americans [Isaac Hecker and myself]. Present him my good wishes and warm love should you fall in his way.

"I have no idea of what is going on in America. Pray, does the good cause make progress? Do the Puseyites convert themselves, or do they take the back track, and swallow down again all the great Catholic sentiments they have been accustomed to utter? God have mercy on them, for it is a fearful thing to approach so near the Holy Ark, and then turn their backs. What is the state of the seminary? Is there still left a leaven of holy mischief, some good seed of truth which gives hope of fruit to the salvation of those poor Anglicans?

"As for my future destiny, you know, of course, that the vow of obedience leaves me no choice. I am at the disposal of my superiors, thank God. I can say, however, that I have commenced a course of theology which will most likely last two years. There is, therefore, little prospect of my returning to America before that time, should I return at all.

"I send you this by means of some of our Fathers who leave very soon for missions in America. My present address is 'Wittem—par Maestricht—Limbourg—Holland. Care of Rev. FF. Redemptorists, etc.'

"The country in which I am resembles very much New England in its scenery. The people are whole-souled Catholics—poor, but full of faith. The little children when they meet us run up to touch our hands with their little hands, esteeming it as a benediction no doubt. Close by us, on the summit of a hill, is a large cross, or crucifix, which can be seen from a great distance, with a 'Way of the Cross' leading up to it, where the people may celebrate the different stations of Our Lord's passion in a manner exceedingly appropriate. I was much struck when I first saw it, and thought of you, who love so much to see such things by the wayside. And now, farewell, my dear friend and brother in Christ! Our sweet Lady guide and protect you always, and build in both our hearts a convent of retirement and contemplation better contrived and better executed than our *quondam* monastery at Wadhams Mills —where she herself may preside as our good Lady Abbess, with Jesus for the great Head of our Order. Your faithful friend and brother in Christ, C. WALWORTH."

Wadhams had been received into the church in June, 1846, by Dr. Peter Fredet, then registrar of the Sulpician Seminary. Father Deluol was president. He received tonsure and minor orders from Archbishop Eccleston, September 2d, 1847. Two years later he was made deacon. He was ordained priest at St. Mary's Pro-Cathedral, Albany, by Bishop McCloskey, January 15th, 1850; and continued to reside in that city, as assistant priest, rector of the Cathedral, and later as vicar-general, until he became Bishop of Ogdensburg.

Although separated from my friend Wadhams by the broad Atlantic for a period of five years, including the whole of his course at the Sulpician Seminary of St. Mary's, Baltimore, two sources of information have just been opened which supply me with some very definite and valuable information concerning his seminary career. Father Griffin, a venerable priest still living at St. Charles' College, Ellicott City, Md., was a companion and intimate friend of Bishop Wadhams while at the seminary. Though now advanced in years and unable to write, he remembers very well the young convert from the Northern Woods, and the olden times when they were together in Baltimore. His reminiscences have been communicated to me, in answer to my written inquiries. I have also letters from the Rev. H. F. Parke. Although, to borrow his own description of himself, "well worn with forty years of mission labors of all sorts—from the Kentucky, Tennessee, and North Carolina to the Mason and Dixon lines"—and now obliged in his old age to lie by as chaplain to the Visitation Convent in Wheeling, West Virginia, Father Parke remembers Wadhams well. He also was his companion at St. Mary's, and "warms up at his name and memory" to send me valuable contributions.

Father Griffin tells us that Wadhams entered the Baltimore Seminary impressed with a feeling that he had come to the source, the centre, the cradle of Catholicity in the United States. He put himself absolutely in the hands of the superior of the seminary, then the Very Rev. Louis Regis Deluol, S.S. I saw Father Deluol at Saint Sulpice, in Paris, early in the winter of 1850. Four Sisters of Charity from the United States dropped in upon us at the same time, and a very lively and delighted American party we made. The picture of the genial and superb old man is strongly impressed upon my memory. In Father Deluol the young neophyte found a pronounced admirer and warm friend. The seminary also numbered among its faculty Messrs. Verot, afterwards Bishop of Savannah, and still later transferred to the see of St. Augustine; Lhomme, who afterwards became president of the seminary; Fredet, then registrar of the seminary, and Dubreuil. Socially and spiritually, therefore, the ex-Anglican deacon could say, as I am told he often did say, *Funes ceciderunt mihi in præclaris.* "He was happy, thoroughly happy," writes Father Parke, "without a doubt or misgiving left to ruffle his peace of mind." The superior placed Wadhams under the instruction of the Rev. Father P. Fredet, D.D., or rather, as they used to say at the seminary, of *Mr. Fredet*. It was evident to him that Wadhams had been already well instructed in the faith before his arrival, and he was, therefore, soon received into the church, and baptized solemnly in St. Mary's Chapel. His kneeling for three years to so austere an ascetic as Fredet in confession—the same priest who reconciled him to the church—gives us an inkling, says Parke, of how bravely he was then travelling in the pathway of the Crucified.

St. Mary's Seminary in Wadhams' time could only accommodate nineteen students. Of these the average attendance in the divinity classes was about twelve; the rest were collegians of the *petit seminaire*, or philosophers.

Among his companions were the late Father Bernard McManus, of St. John's, Baltimore, and the Reverend Francis Boyle, of Washington City. With these for many years Wadhams maintained a long and loving intimacy, frequently visiting and receiving visits from them. To them must be added, besides those already mentioned, John McNally, afterwards pastor of St. Stephen's Church, Washington City; John Henry Walters, of the Wheeling diocese; Francis Xavier Leray, afterwards Archbishop of New Orleans; Jacob Walter, of St. Patrick's Church, Washington City; John Larkin, of New York City; Henry Hennis, of Philadelphia, and William Lambert, of Pittsburgh, brother of Father Lambert, of Waterloo, N. Y. Right Rev. Thomas P. Foley, of Chicago, was ordained in 1846, and must, therefore, have graduated just before Wadhams' arrival. As, however, Mr. Foley continued for some years to reside at Baltimore, becoming vicar-general of the archdiocese, he must be numbered in the group of friends in which Wadhams now mingled, and which helped to develop a character so open to all good influences.

The period of our friend's introduction to this new and valuable circle of friends was a very lively one for the American church, as Father Parke reminds us: "It was the era of Brownson's submission to the church, and of hunger to get hold of his essays. Even the stolid Dr. Fredet enthused over them, and compared their writer to Suarez in breadth and depth of treating his subjects; McMaster from his tripod was making things lively and interesting; while such writers as Martin J. Spalding and Dr. Verot were handling, with gloves off, the *Southern Quarterly Review*, for its defective reviewing of D'Aubigné's *History of the Reformation;* others were canvassing Dr. Jarvis' reply to Milner's *End of Controversy;* while the *United States Catholic Magazine*, edited by the Rev. Charles I. White and M. J. Spalding, later our Archbishop of Baltimore, was then at the height of its usefulness."

Wadhams now found himself in a new world of manly religious thought and sound theology. He had escaped from the sentimental baby-house in which so many Anglicans were amusing themselves. The Catholic thought which now attracted him, and with which his mind was fed, was no longer a diluted water-gruel. His teachers dared to say what they meant, and were not obliged to present the truth in some form of language which left open a safe door of retreat. He was at last free, and felt his emancipation.

I am anxious that Mr. Wadhams should be presented to the reader at this day in the same shape and light in which he appeared so long ago to his new friends at the Catholic Seminary. We will let Father Parke take the stand first. This is his testimony:

"His subdued, manly, dignified bearing, and frank manners, were in his favor from his entrance. Before being a month in the house, the impression made on the superiors and his fellow-students was deep, favorable, and lasting. All were of the belief that Wadhams would stick and prove an acquisition. His profound piety and scrupulous exactitude in observance of rule and addiction to the practices of the interior life, his lightheartedness and capacity to enjoy a joke, and take part in the recreations and sports, soon made him a general favorite."

Father Griffin's memory sees him in the same light. He speaks of him thus:

"Wadhams was a man in every way sincere, who knew no wish but what the world might hear. There was nothing stern about him, but he was always earnest in everything that he undertook. He was remarkable for his regularity in the observance of the rules and every duty. He was a marked man, but without any show of eccentricity. This, however, can be said, that the earnestness and common sense which characterized him were made emphatic by a simplicity of heart and manner that never forsook him.

"In Lent he was a strict observer of the fast, though the observance cost considerably to his nature. In the morning he, as everybody else, took a cup of coffee with a water-cracker the size of a silver dollar. Dinner was at 1.20 o'clock. One day," says Father Griffin, "meeting Wadhams after the teaching of his morning class (about 12.40 o'clock), I asked him: 'How are you, Mr. Wadhams?' With his usual earnest tone, 'Don't talk to me,' said he; 'I feel as if I could *eat brickbats.*'

"He lived in the seminary, but had to teach in the college. With the other seminarians he joined in all the games. He seemed to take much interest in the game of wooden balls. When he made a good play, he would lift his hands vigorously into the air, with an oft-repeated cry of—'Sam Hill! didn't I give a good hit?'

"From the beginning he gained the respect, the esteem, and the good will of the inmates. His name came to be held in benediction among all his friends in the seminary."

In regard to his theological studies, and to his abilities as a teacher in the college, the testimony of Father Griffin is that his success was fair. That his success in study was not rated at more than fair, is not to be attributed to any want of superior intelligence. It came from a defective memory for names and words. This defect attended him through his whole life. It made recitation in class less easy. In particular it made him a poor scholar in languages. Although often obliged to speak in French, especially when travelling abroad or when making visitations in his diocese, he never could master that tongue or indeed any other. This same defect often embarrassed him when meeting with familiar friends. He could not readily recall their proper names and addresses, and was not infrequently obliged to ask for these, to his own confusion. Any one, however, who might be tempted to mistake the want of this particular gift for a lack of keen intelligence, was soon forced to change his mind, on better acquaintance. The distinction which I have just endeavored to make is forcibly brought out by Saintine, in his story of *Picciola*. In speaking of a certain learned man who at the age of twenty-five years had a complete knowledge of seven languages, and was more notable for a love of discussion and quotation than any power of wise observation or reflection, the author remarks: "One can be a fool in several languages." Montalembert had in his mind a similar distinction when, standing in the tribune of the French assembly and seeing around him a voluble crowd of red republican orators, he made them furious by calling them "little rhetoricians" (*petits rhéteurs*).

One thing I deeply regret. I cannot give to the reader not personally and intimately acquainted with Wadhams any just conception of that interior piety which made his life a true walk with God, and which certainly characterized him at St. Mary's Seminary. True, I have quoted the language of witnesses who state this strongly, and I myself might enlarge upon their statements. Statements and enlargements, however, of this kind make little impression upon most readers. The language of eulogy is something so customary, and so freely and largely used, that they give little heed to it, and retain little of it in their memories, except when presented in facts which leave it pictured and framed into a distinct portrait of the man. The witnesses of Wadhams' life at St. Mary's are too few and they are too far away. Even if they were more numerous and nearer, still Wadhams was not a man to talk much about himself, and least of all to talk much of his own emotions or any of that secret intercourse which he held with his Maker. Familiar friends get to know something of this interior life of a good man, but only little by little, and this mostly by inferences drawn from outward actions. Wadhams does not seem to have kept any diary or preserved copies of letters or papers of his own writing. The most sacred and best part of his life is, therefore, the least known to us. This is the great defect of the present "Reminiscences." I feel the defect deeply. It seems to me that I am presenting to the public a caricature of my friend rather than a real likeness. I am forced to dwell upon traits which, although really characteristic, yet belong only to the surface of the man, leaving the deeper and higher soul in shadow. I fear to have dwelt too much upon what is only peculiar, strange, striking, or amusing, rather than what is edifying. I have no excuse but this, that I do my best. To represent a holy soul like Wadhams' truly and adequately would require a spirit like his own. Here, then, I must close this account of his life at Baltimore. It is the best that I can furnish.

Chapter VI.

Wadhams' Priesthood at St. Mary's Church and at the Cathedral, Albany.—The War of the Rebellion.—His Trip to Europe and the Holy Land.

1850–1872.

I PROPOSE to treat the period of my friend Wadhams' priesthood not according to any regular biographical method, but by means of miscellaneous recollections. In this way I shall be able to illustrate more fully than I have yet done not only the spiritual character of the man, but to portray him in the discharge of his official duties and in his more familiar intercourse with others. This I can well afford to do because his career in the priesthood is not so much marked by striking events as by acts and circumstances which reveal his strong personality and the beauty and holiness of his character.

Wadhams was eminently an unconventional man—unconventional in his thoughts, unconventional in his language, unconventional in all his ways. There was an openness and directness in his speech which made many of his sayings peculiar and memorable.

Once when we were passing out from the front

Sexton's House.   St. Mary's Cathedral, Ogdensburg, N. Y.   Rectory.

door of an inn he looked up at the sky and, stopping, said: "Perhaps it may rain; what do you think?" "I don't know," I replied: "let's consider a moment." "Well," said he, "while you are considering, I'll get the umbrella."

Another time when walking up State Street, in Albany, in company with Father Kennedy, then an assistant at St. Mary's and now Vicar-General at Syracuse, who is pretty rapid in his movements, Father Wadhams felt disposed to move more slowly. "Young man," said he, "how long did you tell me you had been in this city?" "About three years," replied Kennedy. "Three years in Albany! and don't know how to walk up-hill yet?" Strangers who have visited Albany will appreciate the force of the question.

Wadhams had a fine musical ear and a great fondness for good ecclesiastical music. Among his manuscripts is an article on Gregorian chant written for the *New York Churchman*, which, perhaps, was never published. He was quite efficient in teaching plain singing and chanting. While officiating in the Anglican church at Ticonderoga, he had a class of boys who assembled at the village inn and learned of him to read music and sing by help of a blackboard. He it was who first introduced in Albany the custom, now universal in all the Catholic churches there, of using the altar-boys to sing the responses at High Mass and to act as chanters in the sanctuary. He loved to attend the rehearsals of these boys at the cathedral. They were always animated by his presence to do their best. "Come now, boys," he would say, "hold up your heads and open your mouths. I don't want any dummies here." And then when their voices rang out clear and loud he would praise them heartily, and they were eager to please him. The regular choir in the Albany Cathedral acquired a high reputation in his time, and they owed it not merely to the great abilities of Mr. Carmody, the organist, but to the great zeal and strong patronage which Wadhams lent to that department of the service.

The popular Christmas carol, "The Snow lay on the Ground," is well known throughout the United States. It is not, however, so well known that we are indebted for it to Bishop Wadhams. He found the verses in some stray newspaper which fell into his hands, and was so pleased with their simple beauty that he was anxious to fit them to some appropriate melody. Father Noethen, of the Holy Cross Church, Albany, to whom he showed the lines, bethought himself of a favorite air of the *Pifferari*, who come in from the Campagna at Christmas time to sing and play in the streets of Rome. His memory of the air was, however, indistinct, and Mr. Carmody was requested to remodel it and adapt it to the words. This he did, and the form he gave to it is the one now universally used. The original air was afterwards procured from Rome, but Mr.

Carmody's variation is adhered to as far more beautiful.

Father Wadhams was an intelligent man, but in our American Church, full of intelligent clergy, that cannot be set down as a distinctive personal peculiarity. The same thing may be said of many other mental qualities of his, most important to prelate or priest, but which cannot be justly alleged as peculiar to him. His great characteristics all lay in the moral order. He was no common man, he was no ordinary priest. All those who knew him well will acknowledge that there was something in him which marked him as eminent. It was a nobility of soul. It was a moral beauty of character. It was a conscience full of power, which would yield to no evil, and before which all evil quailed. Intellect, talent, rank, dignity, all sophistry and all subterfuges, lost their force before him when there was a call upon his conscience to assert itself. There was something magnetic about him, and in this moral energy all the magnetism lay. In ordinary times, however, when conscience was not put in question, he was one of the humblest, simplest, most unpretending and least self-asserting, most yielding, most easily persuaded, of mortals. He was not at all disposed to stand upon his own dignity or to urge his own opinion upon others. On the contrary he was much given to admiration of other men in whom he saw, or thought he saw, remarkable qualities of mind or attractive characteristics. He was, moreover, extremely reticent in expressing disapprobation of the conduct or character of other men where he had no special call to speak or to interfere. My impression of him is that he was not a very quick and close judge of human nature; that he might easily be deceived by those who undertook to do it warily, and was disposed to attribute good motives to all. When, however, aroused to action by some palpable attempt at wrong-doing he was a lion and feared no consequences. I give one instance.

A seminary student had carried his irregularities so far that he was dismissed from the institution. He had friends, however, who were anxious to have him take orders. Great influence to this end was brought to bear upon the bishop. Several persons, on the contrary, ranged themselves stoutly in opposition. Wadhams in particular was so shocked by the very danger of such a thing that he declared his determination, if necessary, to protest publicly against it in the church should the candidate present himself. No measure so strong as this was eventually called for. The bishop, being convinced of the young man's unfitness, refused to admit him to orders. Examples could easily be given where high authority was made to bend in presence of that same lofty and determined conscience.

There was sometimes a certain appearance of antagonism in Wadhams in which his outward ways and language did not always correspond with the qualities of his heart. He had a directness and even bluntness of speech which coming from some persons might easily be taken for rudeness. His friends, however, knew well that it came from the truthfulness and simplicity of his nature, which made it impossible for him to adopt the ways of a courtier by the least evasion of truth. At the same time his heart was full of a kindly charity which, even in little things, made him fearful of giving offence. I will give one or two instances.

On one occasion while he occupied the position of rector of the Albany Cathedral a small party of friends, mostly laymen, were lingering at his room one night after bedtime. He was not fond of late hours, and on this occasion was evidently drowsy. I saw him pacing up and down the room uneasily, and I knew that he was endeavoring to formulate some hint to his friends of his anxiety to retire, and without hurting their feelings. I knew very well what was coming and watched for the result. "Gentlemen," he said at last, as if a happy expedient had just struck him, "I don't know what you are going to do, but I am going to bed." All who were present knew him well, and no one felt in the least hurt.

The world will never remember Wadhams as an eminent preacher. I am confident, however, that in the record of heaven his name will stand in the list of true evangelists. The people who listened to him heard from his lips the true word of God, delivered in simple language, sometimes blunt, sometimes quaint, always unconventional, and oftentimes made powerful and impressive by the very simplicity of the speaker's style, which lent strength to the matter. His was an eloquence which, if it gained nothing from rhetoric, never lost anything through being commonplace. Not knowing of any published sermons of his, I can, unfortunately, give my readers no example to illustrate the spiritual power of his preaching. I fear it will seem something like caricature to confine myself, as I needs must, to its simplicity and originality. He never wasted words in the endeavor to introduce his subject gracefully or conventionally. If the gospel of the day did not suit his purpose, he either took his text elsewhere or, starting from the gospel of the Sunday, he soon landed himself in the field where he proposed to work. One Sunday morning, the fifth after Pentecost, he read the gospel for that day, and then began his sermon as follows:

"It is not unusual to make use of this gospel by preaching on the evil of venial sin. I don't intend to preach this morning on venial sin. I wish to have you all understand that there is a sin which, whether venial or not, is something very ugly and very mischievous. It's a sin to come late to Mass and walk down the broad aisle in fine feathers and fluttering ribbons, as if it were something highly respectable to disturb

public worship by coming late. I do not wish
to be understood as objecting to putting on good
clothes to come to church with, but I do object
to coming late to Mass, to disturbing others who
are praying, and to your making a parade of
yourselves." This is not the form usually pre-
scribed for an exordium, but it certainly led up
to the subject in hand and helped to make the
sermon impressive.

We wish in these reminiscences to make some
mention of Father Wadhams in connection with
the War of the Rebellion, in which he took a
most lively and serious interest. In April, 1861,
when Fort Sumter was attacked, Colonel Michael
K. Bryan was in command of the Twenty-fifth
Regiment, which left Albany immediately for
Washington. On the night of April 21st, 1861,
came the order from Governor Morgan to leave.
The men, mostly workmen, gathered suddenly at
the armory at the tolling of the bells, a signal already agreed upon, and at eight o'clock were all in
line. Their wives and children had only time to
bid them "good-by" at the armory, the hurry not
allowing all of them to go from their workshops
to their homes. Most of the soldiers of this regiment, as well as the colonel and lieutenant-colo-
nel, were Catholics. John M. Kimball, Esq., a
prominent lawyer of Albany, volunteered to go
with them, and received a temporary appointment as chaplain. In any case a departure so
sudden must needs be attended with much con-

fusion, but in this case there existed great excitement throughout the city and an apprehension of imminent danger. The news of the savage assault on a Massachusetts regiment in Baltimore as it marched across the city from station to station, and telegrams on April 19th and 20th, stating that Davis was "within one day's march of Washington with an army," and that troops must hurry on at once or that city would be lost, created a desire in the minds both of Catholic soldiers and their families to prepare for the worst by a due reception of the sacraments. Father Wadhams accordingly offered to accompany the troops, so far as might be necessary, to aid in this preparation.

They started that afternoon, crossing the river by the ferry and taking the cars on the eastern side. Father Wadhams commenced immediately hearing confessions in a corner of one of the cars, a continual silence being maintained on that car until he had finished. Late that night the train, a special and slow one, reached Poughkeepsie, and the good priest, having finished his work, was able to return to Albany. He had found an opportunity in the mean time to receive into the church Counselor Kimball, baptizing him on the train with such water as the drinking-tank contained. Survivors of the regiment assure me that the counselor never officiated as chaplain, though often urged by his gay companions to do so. He did, however, do most serviceable duty as adjutant of the regiment, to which rank he was soon thereafter assigned.

The death of the gallant Colonel Bryan, at Port Hudson, La., was communicated to Father Wadhams in a letter from Dr. O'Leary, surgeon of Bryan's regiment, dated at New Orleans June 18th, 1863. What the good priest's sorrow was at this intelligence may be in some degree gathered from the following passage of the letter: "He lived about an hour after receiving his wounds. He seemed to feel conscious of his approaching end and died like one going to sleep. I have just arrived in this city with his remains and shall send them home at the earliest opportunity." He then adds: "A nobler man never lived. A braver soldier never wielded a sword. A truer Christian never knelt before his Maker."

Although a strong Unionist of the most devoted type, Father Wadhams was always gentle in dealing with soldiers and partisans of the States in rebellion. He could not reconcile himself to their reasonings, but he comprehended very well how much of excusable human nature there was in their sentiments. He was often, however, much shocked even when his gentle nature urged him to keep silence. An Albanian was living in one of the southwestern States before the war, and was a captain there of a well-drilled company of infantry. When the war broke out this company was summoned to arms. It seemed to him a point of honor, and a duty to the company and to the State in which he for the time being resided, to turn out with the rest in the service of the Confederacy. After the war he returned to the North and resided in Albany. Wadhams was surprised one day at hearing it mentioned that this gentleman had been a rebel. "You don't mean to say," he asked, "that you actually fought against us in battle?" "Well, yes," was the reply, "in several battles." "But you didn't kill any of our brave soldiers, did you?" "I can't say, Father, that I did, not exactly; but I will tell you the nearest thing to it that I remember. One day when I was senior captain in command of a regiment, and had my men picketed behind a fence, a troop of Federal cavalry passed by on the road. I gave the order to fire. The consequence was that thirteen saddles in that troop were left empty."

The good Father asked no more questions. He was simply shocked and remained silent, fearing to say too much if he spoke at all. He felt that cruel war bitterly. I often heard him allude to empty chairs at farm-houses in the neighborhood of his own homestead amid the Adirondacks. His nephew Pitt, son of his brother Abraham E. Wadhams, was killed in the war at Chancellorsville.

In 1865 Father Wadhams and his friend, the Rev. William Everett, who, as we have seen, had been his fellow-student at the Twentieth Street Seminary, planned out a journey to be taken together through Europe and to the Holy Land. They met in London and travelled through Paris, Venice, Milan, Rome, and Naples to Egypt and Syria. In Rome they were presented together to His Holiness Pius IX.

A more earnest man than Bishop Wadhams can scarcely be imagined. To his mind duty always rose up above every other consideration. "Faithful and true" were written upon his forehead, where all men could read the inscription; but yet he was light-hearted, joyous, and easily amused, while his laughter was always hearty and perfectly contagious. Father William Everett, on the contrary, his warm and intimate friend, was always as grave and serious in his manner as he was earnest in his soul. This made them sometimes seem strangely mated, the one taking hearty delight in things which the other regarded as trifling. In the course of their journey through Europe Wadhams was interested in almost everything new or strange which presented itself to his eye, while Everett, who had a great taste for Christian archæology, was interested in little else than sacred or historical things. When passing along one of the streets of Turin the former was attracted by an exhibition of Punchinello, and stopped to enjoy it. This mortified Father Everett, who thought it an unseemly thing for clergymen to take interest in a diversion of such a nature. "Do come on," said he; "this is scandalous." "Why, no," said Wadhams, "it's capital!" And he could not be induced to move on. In this he was unexpectedly sustained by two passers-by, old friends of his from Albany, Chancellor Pruyn and his lady, who also stopped to see the show. And thus Everett was compelled to become an unwilling spectator. The two friends prosecuted their journey in company until they reached the Holy Land, which to Everett had always been the main attraction and the chief object of his trip. An account of this visit and of a special pilgrimage to Bethlehem, contributed by Everett himself to *The Catholic World* for 1868, can be found in the January number for that year.

They arrived at Jerusalem in the evening of January 30th, 1866, and were conducted through the darkness, dusty and weary, to the Franciscan hospice. On entering the sitting-room their first surprise was a Troy stove, not calculated certainly to nurse sacred or archæological sentiment in the mind of a student like Everett. There was something else in the apartment quite as American as the Troy heater. It was the figure of a tall, lank man with his hat on his head, his feet projecting above the stove, and smoking a cigar. Removing his cigar, but not either hat or boots, the gentleman turned his head to gaze at the new-comers. They were unmistakably countrymen of his own. "Halloo!" said he, "when did you arrive in Jerusalem?" "We've just come," they replied. "Oh! have you?" said he. "Well then, let me tell you, you've come to one of the most infernal dirty holes that ever *you* saw!" The incongruity of such a welcome to the Holy Land struck Wadhams' sense of the ridiculous, but to the more solemn enthusiasm of his companion such words and the whole scene were a profanation from the shock of which it was not easy to recover.

Their devotion was less disturbed on a visit to Bethlehem, which they made on foot, a distance of about six miles. Here was no Troy stove, nor irreverent Yankee, nor stove-pipe hat, nor profane cigar. They stood under an olive-tree in front of the holy grotto which had served as a shelter to the shepherds when watching their flocks by night. Uncovering their heads devoutly, they chanted the "*Gloria in Excelsis*" with a recollection more tranquil and a joy that could scarcely have been surpassed by that of the shepherds themselves. Wadhams' stay in Jerusalem was short, only a fortnight; but this was not enough to satisfy an archæological pilgrim like Everett, who remained much longer. When returning to the United States the latter brought back many choice reminiscences of the Holy Land, books, maps, illustrations, charts, and plans in relief, rarely to be met with. These were for a long time a source of interest and pleasure to friends of a like taste when, in New York, they visited the rectory of Nativity Church.

Father Wadhams' large heart, less interested in sacred scholarship, was nevertheless equally full of devotion, and full also of the thought of friends. Every beautiful object that met his eye struck him as an appropriate present for some friend at home. He brought back with him a large extra trunk filled with these souvenirs, collected from various places. If it were possible for me to remember the names of all the parties whom he had thus specially borne in mind when abroad and to whom he brought back some appropriate gift, it would seem almost incredible. His brethren of the clergy, members of the cathedral congregation and of St. Mary's, singers in the choir, sacristan, altar-boys, and all the domestics of the house, a very multitude, had something in that trunk to show that they had been remembered. How he managed without the help of saddle-bags to carry so many objects of devotion, rosaries, crucifixes, medals, images, etc., into the presence of the Holy Father to be specially blessed and indulgenced by him, is a wonder which I cannot explain.

There are some men who will never allow that they have changed their opinions. Father Wadhams was not one of this kind. It cost him very little to say: "I used to think so, but I was mistaken." He was always equally ready to acknowledge any moral wrong or defect in what he himself had done. On one occasion, when rector of the Albany Cathedral, the house was disturbed at night by an intoxicated man who would not leave when ordered away, but continued to ring

ST. MARY'S SCHOOL, OGDENSBURG, N. Y.
Built by Bishop Wadhams.

the bell and pound at the door. He claimed that his wife was sick and that the priest must come immediately, but his answers to inquiries showed that his senses were very much confused. Being compelled to rise and dress himself in order to quiet the disturbance, Father Wadhams descended to the hall with hat, overcoat, and cane. Opening the front door, he seized the fellow by his collar, dragged him down the steps and along the pavement as far as the first corner, thrashing him in the mean time with his cane. The man cried out lustily. A policeman coming up and seeing what was the matter said, "Can I help you any, Father?" "No," was the answer, "I can dispose of this job myself." Leaving his prisoner, however, at the corner Father Wadhams did not venture to return to the house without first making sure of the condition of the woman reported as sick. He found her, as he had supposed, in no need of a priest and full of regret at the trouble which her husband had caused. "I am glad to know," she said, "that you gave him a good beating. He deserved it well. The longer the marks of your cane stay on his back the better. It may bring the grace of God down on his foolish head to remember the holy hands that did it." Father Wadhams always regretted this night's adventure. When some of his household sought to justify what had been done, saying that the fellow had deserved it richly, he said: "No, that will not answer. I have done wrong. It was far more important for me to control my own temper than to chastise a turbulent drunkard."

Our reminiscences would be like Italy with Rome left out if we were to say nothing of that charity which was the ruling spirit of Father Wadhams. He maintained it with a singular forgetfulness of himself. As a man he lived for others. As a friend he never forgot the claims of friendship. As a Christian he always saw Christ in the pleading faces of the poor. As a minister of Christ he never forgot that great ruling principle, which he always taught and always followed himself, that "the priest is for the people, not the people for the priest." His charity was always toned and colored by that guilelessness which so peculiarly characterized him. His own simplicity and singleness of heart made him unsuspicious of others. As a natural consequence he was easily imposed upon by strangers, taking for granted that others were as sincere as himself. What we mean, then, will be easily understood when we say that he carried charity to a fault. If the honest poor could count upon his generosity, others less honest could often play upon his simplicity. During his absence in Europe in 1865 I occupied his place temporarily as rector at the Albany Cathedral. I found that by his arrangement the money received in the poor-boxes was divided every week by the sacristan among a number of poor persons. Having some

Residence of Bishop Wadhams, Ogdensburg, N. Y.

suspicion in regard to the wise application of this money, I got a list of these people, which I submitted to the St. Vincent de Paul Society, asking them to report what they knew or could learn of the character of these pensioners. The report was unfavorable to the whole list. Either they were quite capable of taking care of themselves, or could not safely be trusted with money. They were, therefore, all dropped from the list. Only one, an old man, appealed from the sacristan to me. Father Wadhams, he said, had always allowed him his weekly dole of twenty-five cents, and why should it be kept from him now? I answered that it was known to me that he had enough to live upon without it. "Well," he replied, "that's partly true. It's not a necessity, but it was a convenience. It was just enough to supply me with tobacco." It would be needless to enlarge upon the great number of worthier objects of charity to whom living was made easier and happier by the same bountiful hand.

What Shakespeare makes Othello say of himself may, nevertheless, be well applied to the open-hearted and guileless subject of these memoirs. He was—

> "One not easily jealous, but being wrought,
> Perplexed in the extreme."

Duplicity, fraud, treachery, once detected in one to whom he had given his confidence, there came a shock from which he could not easily recover and give a second confidence. He and I had both formed a very favorable opinion of a priest of the diocese, chiefly derived from a certain appearance of modesty and ecclesiastical dignity which we saw in him. Father Wadhams, from holding the administration of the diocese for a while during the bishop's absence, was brought to know of many things in the conduct of this man, some of which showed moral weakness only, but other things hypocrisy, treachery, and a fraudulent avarice. Wadhams brought him to bay and hunted him out of the diocese with an inflexibility and rapidity of action which astonished me.

He was once visited by a newspaper reporter, who did not announce himself as such, but came to the house in the character of a fellow-citizen who was anxious to make his acquaintance. He talked so pleasantly and cheerfully that Wadhams was highly entertained, and talked very freely in return. He was much disconcerted shortly after on finding the conversation reported in a daily newspaper, containing many things not well adapted for publication. Before his indignation had time to cool the visitor most unwisely called again. A rapid retreat through the front door became necessary, and terminated the intercourse. I do not remember the precise words which my friend used on this occasion, but they were perfectly intelligible and brief. In substance they were like those of Lady Macbeth when dismissing her guests from the banquet table: "Stand not upon the order of your going, but go at once!"

The purity of Father Wadhams' character amounted to a degree of delicacy which is rare even among the virtuous. I recall the modesty which pervaded his manners and language as something truly angelic. In all my reminiscences of him, which reach through so many years of intimacy, embracing often circles where the most free and joyous conversation abounded, I never heard a word from his lips suggestive even of that *stultiloquium* so strongly condemned by the Apostle Paul, and so especially unworthy of the lips of a priest. It was so before he became a Catholic, it was so before my acquaintance with him began. It was so from his boyhood up. No one that ever knew him well can doubt that his very soul was virginal. An old friend and school-companion of his gives his testimony to this feature of his character in the following words:

"During his whole college life, I, who knew him better than any other human being all that time could know him, know that he never spoke one impure word or said anything that a man would be ashamed to repeat in the presence of his mother, sister, or niece. I am to-day a better man than I should have been had I not been intimate with Wadhams."

I might easily suppose this trait to be due to a certain excellence of nature. Perhaps it was. The friend just cited, however, seems to regard it as a gift of grace, for he says: "He was truly a devout man even from youth up."

If in these reminiscences my main purpose has been successful, I have shown that Wadhams was in no sense an ordinary man. I do not mean to assert that all his talents and qualities of heart were above mediocrity. I mean only that he was in no way commonplace, neither in thought nor manner nor language. I attribute this to the fact that he was too truthful and simple-hearted to borrow nonsense from any source, however conventional or popular the nonsense might be.

Lacordaire was accustomed to say: "*Je n'aime pas les lieux communs.*" I don't remember ever to have heard Father Wadhams say this. It was true of him all the same. His ways, thoughts, and feelings were all his own, all unborrowed. He was, therefore, in no sense a commonplace man.

Chapter VII.

Wadhams becomes Bishop of Ogdensburg.—His Life and Labors in the New Diocese.—His Sufferings and Sudden Cure.—Trials.—His Last Illness and Death.

1872–1891.

NEAR the close of the year 1871 it had become evident that a division of the diocese of Albany was called for. The Right Rev. John J. Conroy assembled the Councilors of the diocese, and represented to them that such was the fact. He asked them to advise with him as to the character and qualities of the man who should be recommended to the Holy See for the new diocese, and also as to what place should be selected as the proper seat or see for the residence of the new bishop. The diocese itself was to consist of the Adirondack region, including the plains which border this region on the north and west. Only two towns sufficiently populous for this purpose could be considered as sufficiently central. The one was Plattsburgh, on Lake Champlain, and the other Ogdensburg, in the northwest at the point where the Oswegatchie River connects with the Saint Lawrence. The sentiments of the council were very nearly equally divided as to the location of the see.

A bishop's council had no claim at that time to make a nomination, nor was any name suggested. The principal point on which the opinion of the council was desired was the following, namely: What should be the nationality of the man to be recommended? This was a point of no little importance, for the English language was by no means universal in Northern New York, especially among Catholics. Many Canadians had settled there, and their number was constantly increasing. The opinion nearly, if not quite unanimous, was that the new bishop should understand French, but that his native and most familiar tongue should be English.

Ogdensburg was designated by the authorities at Rome as the seat of the new see, and the name of the new bishop was communicated to Father Wadhams by Archbishop McCloskey in the following note:

"NEW YORK, February 25th, 1872.

"RIGHT REV. DEAR SIR: I am instructed by the Cardinal Prefect of the Propaganda to make known to you the fact that you have been appointed by the Holy Father to the new see of Ogdensburg. The apostolic letter and other documents were in course of preparation, and will be expedited with as little delay as possible. My secretary, Dr. McNeirny, who will present you

this, has been appointed coadjutor bishop of Dr.
Conroy. Permit me to present you my most sincere congratulations as well as my best wishes and
regards. Commending myself to your prayers,
"I remain, monsignor,
"Very truly your friend and brother in Christ,
"JOHN, *Abp. of New York.*"

The bulls arrived in due course of time, and
the bishop-elect prepared for his consecration.

The Rev. Edgar P. Wadhams was consecrated
bishop by Archbishop McCloskey (the assistant
consecrators being Bishops De Goesbriand, of
Burlington, and Williams, of Boston) on the fifth
day of May, 1872, at the Albany Cathedral, amid
a throng of spectators. Many of these were old
friends—bishops, priests, and laymen—who had
come from a distance to witness this ceremony.
The great multitude, however, were citizens of
Albany, who knew and loved him well.

Among these was an old friend and comrade
who had been selected by the bishop-elect to
preach at his consecration. He struck a keynote on that occasion when, before concluding
his sermon, he said:

"A friend is about to say FAREWELL. Thirty
years ago, when my eyes were brighter and my
footsteps lighter, I entered the halls of a well-known seminary in the city of New York. Coming there as a perfect stranger, I found myself
in a new world and surrounded by strange faces.

With one face, however, I soon became familiar; and ever since, through a checkered and eventful life, at almost every winding of my pathway that same kind face has met me, cheered me, and helped to lighten up the road before me. From that day until this morning, when you have seen him kneeling to receive the consecrating oils, thirty changeful winters have passed over his head, but in him I see no shadow of change. It must be that great development has taken place in many respects; it must be that secret graces have been accumulating; but I see no change in character. Such as he was, so is he now; so, doubtless, will he always be. . . .

"I have been familiar with Edgar Wadhams in youth and in riper manhood. I have seen him in the pursuits of his vocation, busy in the affairs of life, and mingling among men. I have seen him at home among his native Adirondacks, surrounded by the same faces that beamed upon his childhood. And here as well as there, and everywhere, the testimony of all that ever knew him is the same, '*Faithful and True.*' I have seen him in every occupation and mood of mind—in labor, in study, in prayer, in the hour of light-hearted gayety, in sorrow and in joy, groping in the midst of doubt and perplexity, or walking free again in the light of a clear path. These are the natural vicissitudes of life. They come and go; they are themselves subject to change, but they bring no change to a steadfast soul like his. They pass over and leave it, as the clouds float over the face of the constant moon, and leave her as before, still travelling on her heavenly track—*'Faithful and True.'* So has he always been in all the relations of life—as son, brother, friend, Christian, pastor; at his own fireside, at the sickbed, at the altar; and who doubts that in the episcopate, to which God has now called him, he will not be found the same—*'Faithful and True'* to the end? . . .

"Go forth, then, man of God, where God and duty call thee! Be thou the Apostle of the American Highlands, and of that broad and noble plain whose borders are a majestic lake, a mighty river, an inland ocean, and the primeval mountains. Go plant the cross of Christ among thy native hills; unfurl the Catholic banner on the banks of the St. Lawrence and on the shores of Ontario and Lake Champlain; and there where early missionaries, sighing out their holy lives and writing their names in blood, could only save a few scattered souls, do thou in happier times found churches, and convents, and schools! Go, and God's richest blessings go with thee! But be sure of this: wherever thou goest and whatever new friends may gather around thee, in the broad field of thy new mission thou wilt find none to love thee better, none truer, than those thou leavest now in tears and sadness behind thee!"

Some of Bishop Wadhams' familiar friends in

Albany were anxious to retain a photograph of him before he left for his new scene of labor, and wished that this picture should represent him in his character of bishop. He very readily consented, and I was delegated to go with him to the photographer. Previous photographs had proved to be more realistic than artistic, presenting him in a dress somewhat awry; wearing, for example, a biretta with a vicious inclination toward one or the other eye. His friends wished me, therefore, to accompany him and keep him in good artistic shape. This was really a necessary precaution. He was very fond of solemnities and religious ceremonies of the highest order. He loved to see rich vestments. All this, however, was for the honor of God and to make divine worship impressive. Outside of the church and moving in the world he concerned himself very little about his personal appearance. He possessed a native dignity peculiarly his own; but he was not at all aware of it and let it take care of itself. When arrived at the photographer's gallery he allowed me to place him and pose him at discretion. His humility and simplicity of heart were proof against all temptations, and whatever his other friends may have thought of the result, he himself was, as usual, perfectly satisfied with the photograph. It would have been hard, indeed, for us all if we could have retained nothing of him in Albany except what a photographer's art can supply, but the city is still full of more truthful reminiscences which cannot easily be obliterated.

We must now follow the new bishop to his see. "It was my pleasure," said Bishop McQuaid in his funeral sermon on Bishop Wadhams, "and my honor to come with him to this infant church of Ogdensburg, just born into the rank of an episcopal city. I remember well that day—the joy of priests and people, and the welcome every one gave him."

The first care of a bishop in taking possession of a newly established see is to arrange a domicile for himself and a cathedral church. But here Bishop Wadhams encountered at once an embarrassment which only a gentleness of heart and a Christian charity like his would have disposed of as he did.

At the time of his appointment to the See of Ogdensburg the charge of the church and the congregation there was in the hands of an old and excellent priest, who had devoted himself to it and had done the best he could to bring it to a flourishing condition. The old priest occupied, of course, the parish house adjoining, and it never occurred to his mind that it would be necessary to hand over either church or rectory to the new bishop, or to take any subordinate place under him. The good father announced the bishop's arrival to his people as follows (of course I can only give the substance of his words): "You all know, my dear brethren," he said, "that for many long years I have desired and asked for and prayed for a coadjutor. God knows I needed help, but could not get it. At last a coadjutor has arrived and now things will go on better." The new bishop scrupled to dislodge the good old man, and preferred for the moment to take another house for himself, although no other could be found convenient to the church. He said Mass on week-days at a private oratory in the new house, officiating at the church only on Sundays and holidays. He satisfied himself for the time with the supervision of the general affairs of the diocese, trusting that local matters at Ogdensburg would soon arrange themselves little by little and naturally. They did not, however, so arrange themselves. The former incumbent showed no inclination to yield up any part of his responsibilities or allow the bishop to do anything but "coadjute." Things went on in this way for a long while, causing the bishop great uneasiness and inconvenience. On his visiting me one day at St. Mary's, Albany, I expressed my wonder that he should allow things to go on in this way, when it would be so easy for him to set them right and at once. "Yes," he replied, "so it would be, and if he were a different sort of man I would not hesitate for a moment; but just look at the thing as it is. He is a good man, he is a faithful priest; the building up of that congregation has been the work of his life; it would break the poor old man's heart to dislodge him;

and even if he were to stay there and work in the parish under me, it would be a constant and bitter grief to him to see me make the changes which I should think necessary in the church and in the house, and to be obliged to help me in making those changes. Walworth, I can't do it with a good conscience. I cannot trample out that good man's life. I must let things go on as they are until God opens for me a good opportunity to interfere." And he kept steadfastly to this resolution.

"I remember well," said Bishop McQuaid in the funeral sermon already quoted, "I remember well the poverty in which he found his diocese, and the poverty of the city of Ogdensburg. I remember this and other occasions when he unburdened his soul to me and told me of his difficulties, and spoke of his diocese and his people, and their poverty. He spoke of their being scattered over this vast territory, and I listened with feeling and attention to him. With the kindness of a child, he said how he would lead the way, how he was going to change the character of his city and church; and when I looked at the old church, I wondered how the ingenuity of man could turn it into anything that would make it presentable as a cathedral. . . . I listened to him as he spoke of those woods and the people who were scattered through them, whom he said should belong to God's church, and with the utmost joy told me that they were opening up the

North Woods; they were opening railroads into them, etc. Civilization was making rapid strides into the wilderness. . . ."

The separate house he selected for his own residence at the time of his arrival, the only one he could find, was located at a distance from the church. It was a corner house, sufficiently ample, but he could only obtain possession of a part of it. He was soon obliged to remove to a plain frame house near by. Later on he found means to return to his first location, purchasing the whole lot and enlarging the building. Here he remained until his death. This residence is a fine, well-built, and solid edifice, but its furniture was very plain and simple, and cost the bishop very little. The two-ply ingrain carpet which he put down on his first arrival was still there when he died nineteen years later. To his own mind, however, everything was perfectly elegant. Although actually poor, he always seemed to feel himself quite rich, and no one could be more hospitable. The priests who came to him from different parts of his diocese always found a plate at his table, and a room to lodge in.

Although to a man who objected to all luxury, and required so little for his own comfort, the sense of personal poverty was something unknown, yet he had a clear perception of the poverty of his diocese, and was often made to feel it keenly. Once after his appointment and before his consecration, while walking with Professor Carmody on the Kenwood road, he opened his mind to his friend after this manner:

"I know, Carmody, the task I have before me. I know that country well. The population is poor and scattered. It is a land of small settlements and long distances. The people cannot be reached by railways or stage-coaches. Even good wagon-roads are few. But I'll tell you what I mean to do. I shall get a good pony that will carry me anywhere; and you take my word for it, it will not be long before I visit every family; and every man and woman, barefooted boy, and yellow-headed girl in my diocese will know me. Yes, sir-ee!"

I have heard it said, and it may be true, that Bishop Wadhams was not originally designated for Ogdensburg, but for another diocese; and that the appointment which he actually received was owing to the mistake of a clerk at Rome, who filled up a blank with his name where another name should have been entered. However this may be, it is certain that he had some characteristics which fitted him peculiarly for a bishopric among the Adirondacks. He was strong, healthy, and inured to physical fatigue. He was by nature and by training a child of the woods and mountains, the snows and floods. This made him well pleased with the location of his new field of labor. A familiar associate and co-laborer of Wadhams at the Albany Cathedral brings out this thought very happily in a sermon preached at his "month's mind:"

"At the time of his appointment to Ogdensburg," said Bishop Ludden, of Syracuse, "I was present when some person asked him whether he would accept or not. 'How can you,' they said to him, 'leave this great centre of life and go away to that barren and trackless region?' His answer was: 'My dear friends, that is my native air; I love those Adirondacks—I love those mountains, those rivers and streams; I love all there is in that territory. I love to hear the sawmills: they are music to my ears. Why, I was brought up on saw-logs!'"

And so he was. I myself have seen him walking over a fleet of logs that lay moored in a milldam. But although they dipped and turned under his feet, he trod among them as fearless and secure as if he were making his way along a sidewalk. It was his own impression that he knew every tree in the North Woods and could tell its name. When in the forest he walked like a master in his own house, and nature seemed to recognize him as such.

> "He was the heart of all the scene;
> On him the sun looked more serene;
> To hill and cloud his face was known,
> It seemed the likeness of their own;
> They knew by secret sympathy
> The public child of earth and sky."

If Wadhams was a true child of nature, nature

had not given to this child a realistic head or a realistic heart. No one can say of him,

> "A primrose by the river's brim
> A simple primrose was to him,
> And nothing more."

Nature talked to him like a mother, and he responded to her like an eager child. If the Angelus bell is now heard in so many parts of the North Woods it is due to him. I have already spoken of him as a musician. I don't remember that I have mentioned how fond he was of bell-music. To this predilection of his is due the beautiful chime of bells in the cathedral tower at Albany. It was at one time a fond hope of his to introduce a true system of chiming, something quite different from the prevailing practice of banging out hymn-tunes on reluctant bells. He purchased rare books on bell-music, and loved to talk about peals, bobs, triple-bobs, and bob-majors. To this same fondness for bells is due also the fact that the region of the North Woods, and the level belt of land which so nearly surrounds them, has been made vocal thrice in the day with the sound of the *Angelus*.

He was on a visit one day to a parish among the mountains where the prospect was very fine but the grazing very poor. The worthy incumbent found it hard to keep the church in repair, and to keep either church or house warm during the long and cold winters. He did it indeed, but he had to work hard for it. The bishop said to him: "My dear father, you have a bell on your church, but I don't hear the Angelus ring." "No, bishop," the priest replied, "that's so; but in truth we are too poor." "What!" said the bishop, "too poor to ring the Angelus?" "Yes; I can't do it myself with any regularity, and there is no one here who can afford to do it without being paid. You see I am obliged to be my own sacristan, and when I am absent my cook takes charge of the church; but she has already all the work she wants to do." "Call her here," said the bishop. The woman soon presented herself. "Margaret," said the bishop, "have you got so much to do that you could not ring the Angelus three times every day?" "I could, my lord, and will, if you wish it." "You are the right sort of girl for me! Do it then, and keep it up, and you shall have two dollars a month extra."

Some time afterwards this priest came to Ogdensburg on parochial business, and said to the bishop in course of conversation: "I suppose you remember my cook, Margaret? She prays for you every day since your last visit to us." "Good!" said the bishop, "and does she get the two dollars extra?" "Indeed she does," was the reply; "she don't forget that." "And does she keep the bell going every day?" "Indeed she does; that's something I don't forget." "Good for both of you!" said the bishop, slapping his broad hand on the table. "Now I'm satisfied." "Yes," said the priest, "but Margaret is not entirely satisfied. She wants a photograph of yourself, with your autograph on the back of it, and she asked me to tell you that she don't want one of the little things that get mislaid, but she wants a large-sized cabinet." "Glory! Alleluia!" said the bishop, starting to his feet and clapping his hands together. "She shall have one as big as the side of a house, if she wants it! But let her keep that bell going."

It may easily be imagined, even by those who do not know the fact statistically, that the diocese of Ogdensburg made progress during the nineteen years of Bishop Wadhams' episcopate. New parishes were formed, new churches built, schools were established, priests were added to the clergy list, convents were founded, and the number of Catholic population increased. In a country like ours all these things take place naturally, no matter who the bishop may be. Catholics and Catholic institutions augment necessarily with the growth of the country. All this increase cannot be set down as a development of organic life. Much of it is only concretionary. Much of it even remains a mere drift or detritus. To turn all this swelling tide of life to good account, to the glory of God and the salvation of men, requires hard and constant missionary labor, the tribute of faithful and earnest hearts. Bishop Wadhams looked with joy upon the growth and improvement in his diocese, but he was too truthful and too humble to take all the credit of it to himself, and remain unmindful that the largest part of this was the work of his clergy, and he was always careful to give the principal credit of it to them and others who labored with them.

In July, 1890, when on a visitation to Port Henry, he was greeted with a complimentary address by the sodalities of St. Patrick's parish. In this address much was said of the growth of the diocese under his administration, which was attributed simply to his personal zeal and labor. The growth of the diocese was a thought in which the good bishop took great delight. The tribute to himself did not please him so well. After complimenting the address as something very beautiful and very grateful to his feelings, he said:

"You speak of the diocese. No doubt you know a great many things about the diocese. There may be some things, however, that you do not know. I can give you some statistics. I found the diocese with forty priests, and now there are seventy-six. I found fifteen, perhaps twenty—no more—religious women in the diocese. Now there are considerably over a hundred teaching, some seven or eight employed in our orphan asylum and hospital in Ogdensburg as a beginning—but all the rest, you may say, teaching. What you attribute to me, however, must be passed over to the credit of the priests of the diocese, of each one of them. It reflects to the credit of the religious orders—the religious men, the sisters. It reflects to the credit of the laity; of young women like you, the Children of Mary, members of the Rosary Society and other Sodalists; married women also, and married men, all full of devotion, all working together for the poor, for the church, in union and charity with each other and in unity with the Vicar of Christ. That's what makes things grow!"

That same open, unmasked, guileless character which had endeared Bishop Wadhams to the people of Albany drew also all hearts to him in Ogdensburg. A movement was set on foot there by his fellow-citizens to celebrate the eighteenth anniversary of his consecration by a public ovation. It was well known that the humble prelate was as little fond of ovations as he was of presents, and they would gladly have made it "a surprise party," but it was not easy in such a town to take him by surprise. It was necessary to secure his consent. A committee was therefore appointed to wait on him and tender him a public banquet. The bishop was embarrassed. His heart was as genial as it was humble. And then, again, there is never more danger of giving offence than when kindness is not met cordially. He got out of the embarrassment in this way. "I see, I see," he said. "What you propose is an anniversary banquet. Thank you; thank you. That would be glorious. You shall have it.

You will come to my house on the fifth, all of you—the more the merrier—and we will have a big supper. I will provide the entertainment. Leave that to me." And so it was done, the bishop taking all the expense on himself. One of the Protestant gentlemen present caused much merriment by reporting to the bishop the remark of a beggar whom he had found perched on the steps at the entrance. "Isn't it a fine thing to be a bishop, sir!" said he. The bishop enjoyed this as a capital joke, and it is needless to say that the beggar lost nothing by it.

This is nearly the old familiar story of the Irishman who said, as he leaned upon his spade: "Laboring work is not that bad after all; but for a nate, dacent, aisy job give me a bishop!"

The good citizens of Ogdensburg, who had plotted this feast as an honor to a man they admired, were not disposed to be outwitted after this sort. They therefore got up among themselves a purse to defray the expense and sent it to the bishop. The bishop was surprised, but not outwitted. His delicacy would not allow him to send the purse back. He saved, however, his personal independence and maintained his known aversion to public honors and to receiving costly presents for his own use, by hastening to apply the contents of this purse to the decoration of his cathedral. The handsome draperies, red and gold, which were then placed in the sanctuary, still hang there, bearing witness how well the good bishop understood the danger of those public flatteries called testimonials, the natural influence of which is to poison the heart and bind the hands of the recipient. Father Conroy not long after, taking advantage of the bishop's absence, pointed to these decorations from the pulpit and said to the people: "It is like everything he does, what is his is ours."

Perhaps no better place can be found to introduce an anecdote which illustrates a certain moral majesty which often invested the person of Bishop Wadhams, and which was sometimes awakened by the very sound of his voice. A burglar once broke into his house after midnight when the household were all asleep. He entered the bishop's room, whose slumber was not so deep as to prevent his awaking.

"Who is that?" said he in a gentle voice. "Is it you, Father Byrnes?" naming one of the household who was ill at the time. There was no answer. The bishop then demanded more sternly, "Who is that, I say?" "I am a burglar," was the unexpected reply. "Oh, you are a burglar, are you?" said the bishop, quietly. "How did you get into the house?"

"By the back door."

"By the back door, eh! Well, that's the wrong door to come into a bishop's house by. Do you know you are in a bishop's bedchamber now?" (No answer.) "Stay where you are for the present. I want to have a little talk with you."

The bishop then proceeded to dress himself partially, after which he struck a light. Then, with the candle in his hand, he proceeded to inspect the person of the burglar, who stood overawed and trembling before him. Perceiving that the man was barefooted, the bishop inquired, "Where are your shoes?"

"I left them at the door when I entered."

"Well, then, come downstairs with me and show me where you left them." The shoes were found standing inside of the back door, as the burglar had reported.

"Now then," said the bishop, "sit down on that chair and put on your shoes." The burglar did as he was ordered and then, all abashed, turned to leave the house by the same way that he had entered, but the bishop held him back.

"No, sir," he said. "I can't allow strangers to leave this house by the back door. Come with me." The burglar followed him to the front door, which the bishop unlocked and opened.

"One word more, my friend," he said. "Have you taken anything belonging to this house?" The burglar showed him his empty hands.

"Have you put nothing in your pocket?"

"Nothing, bishop, nothing — so help me God!"

"Well, good-night, my friend! But see here. The next time you come to visit me, come to this door and ring the bell."

The strange man disappeared in the darkness and was never seen in the neighborhood again.

I give the following incident to show certain traits in the character of Bishop Wadhams which, if not of the highest consequence, were very noticeable and will remain imprinted in the memory of those who knew him. It shows especially the warmth of his natural affections, with a self-forgetfulness and a simplicity of action which readily threw off the restraints of conventional and artificial life.

He was engaged one afternoon in giving confirmation to a class of children, with some adults, at a settlement in the Adirondacks called Bloomingdale near Saranac Lake. Just as he was about to begin the ceremony he saw, to his great surprise, sitting on one of the benches before him a sister of his whom he had not seen for many years. "Why," he said, "is that you?" Overjoyed at the sight, and quite forgetful of all other surroundings, he stepped forth from the sanctuary into the aisle all vested as he was, and with his mitre on, and throwing his arms about her saluted her with a hearty kiss. It then broke upon his mind that he had done something unusual. "Don't be scandalized," he said to the congregation, "it's my sister! My own dear old sister! She has come all the way from California! I haven't seen her for years." And the congregation were not at all scandalized. Simple-hearted as they were and all unartificial, they were more edified by this sudden display of natural affection than they would have been if they had seen the good bishop giving the "Pax" to his assistant priest at the altar in the midst of a pontifical High Mass, and with all the solemn dignity intended by the rubric.

Bishop Wadhams was never a society man, and it was not at all in his nature to become very conventional in his ways and manner. He was, however, a thorough gentleman in all that such a term implies of true courtesy and consideration for others. I give one instance.

Near the close of his life, but before his last illness, old age and increasing infirmity made it difficult for him to dress without assistance. This office was commonly performed by a laboring man in his service named John, whose duty it also was to attend to the fires. One morning when this man came into his room the bishop felt it necessary to take John to task for *malfeasance* in office.

"You neglect the fires, John," he said. "The house is too cold; I feel it and the whole household suffers from it." John took the reproof humbly and quietly, only taking advantage of a short pause to say, "Did you have a good sleep last night, bishop?" Being determined to make an impression on the mind of his attendant the bishop continued to enlarge upon the matter. When this was over John only replied, "Is there any other matter, sir, you'd like to mention?"

"No," was the reply, "you may go now.—Yes, wait a moment!" Then, after a short pause, the bishop continued: "John, when you came into my room a little while ago you wished me good-morning; I forgot to return the salute. Afterwards you asked me if I had had a good sleep; I forgot to answer that also. I found fault with you instead, and you never said a word or looked sullen. John, I can't afford to let you be more of a gentleman than I am. Good-morning to *you*, John. Did I have a good sleep? No, I had a very bad night of it. No fault of yours, though. And now you may go, John, and God bless you."

What the bishop was in his household such he was in his whole diocese and in all his intercourse with the world. He was as much of a gentleman with the least of his inferiors as he was with any of those who ranked above him.

A bishopric in the hands of a man who devotes himself earnestly and conscientiously to his high office involves a life of constant labor, and that a labor attended by many and constant embarrassments. Bishop Wadhams was not a man to shrink from labor. He was a hardy man, both in body and mind, and found happiness in his work. The greatest trouble which his diocese gave him was not from the tax it necessarily made upon his physical powers or mental faculties. It was a pain, and the pain lay at his heart. The pain came when he saw manifested in the flock committed to him anything like discordant feeling or bitterness of contention.

Whatever mischiefs may have hitherto existed in our American Church, its past records will show very little of the spirit of disunion. The clergy have been loyal to their bishops, the congregations have been loyal to their pastors, and the people have dwelt together in a brotherhood of true Christian love. It is manifest, however, that latterly with a change in sources of immigration, which, instead of flowing in one or two large streams, is now fed by a great variety of springs from all parts of Europe, extending even into western Asia, a new condition of things has been engendered. A jarring of nationalities shows itself, all claiming the privilege of engrafting into this country, into its social life, and into the very worship and government of our church, their several peculiarities. These alien elements are not only calculated to disturb and displace what they find here, but they jostle with each other, and they constitute a great practical problem to be solved by our church in our day.

The diocese of Ogdensburg has had its own share in these difficulties, and the heart which most keenly felt the strain has been the great, loving heart of the late Bishop of Ogdensburg. Toward the close of his life his increasing infirmities caused him to apply to the Holy See for a coadjutor. This excited a contention, and the nationality of the proposed coadjutor was the subject of the contention. The trouble assumed such proportions that the wearied bishop finally decided that the wisest course was to withdraw the application and endeavor to bear his burden alone. It is not my purpose to enlarge any further upon this matter. I have only introduced it as a matter too real and too important to be entirely suppressed, and because it will throw light upon the closing scene of the good bishop's life, now soon to be recorded.

Some twelve years after his elevation to the episcopate Bishop Wadhams was attacked by a complication of physical disorders which were not only extremely painful, but interfered with the prosecution of his duties, and even threatened his life. Feeling that a serious crisis was at hand, he came quietly and unannounced to Albany, and, taking a room at St. Peter's Hospital, he placed himself under the care of Dr. Keegan, a visiting physician of that institution, in the hope that a period of quiet rest and skilful treatment might fit him again for active labor.

The sufferings of Bishop Wadhams at this hospital before obtaining relief were, according to Dr. Keegan, as dreadful as human nature can experience. He found him at one time sitting doubled up on his bed in a perfect agony of pain, covered with perspiration, shaking from head to foot and sobbing like a child. "Don't think hard of me, doctor," he said, "to see me cry in this way. I can't help it. I am only a man.

Nothing either more or less." During all the time of his illness, however, he never uttered a word of impatience or complaint. Only the body was shaken. The soul was steadfast. "I recognized at once," said the doctor, "that I had under my hands no common man. He was a man of heroic mould."

The relief obtained from the skilful treatment received in Albany at St. Peter's Hospital, although most serviceable and for the time effectual, did not amount to a permanent cure. The effectual and permanent cure came on the 8th of December, 1886, the feast of the Immaculate Conception. At half-past six o'clock on the morning of that day he celebrated Mass in his private chapel. This Mass was the concluding exercise of a novena which he had instituted to obtain a cure from heaven. The sisters of the Sacred Heart Academy ("Gray Nuns," so called) had at his request taken part in the novena, and were present at the Mass. The disease left him suddenly at the consecration of the Sacred Host, and never returned again. He became overpowered and burst into tears, which flowed abundantly during the remainder of his Mass, but at the end he could not control his feelings and gave full vent to them. He continued at prayer in the chapel until half-past nine. Two of the sisters remained with him there. Several times he said to Sister Stanislaus: "O my child, if I could only tell you what the Immaculate Queen has done for me! I, so unworthy!" This he repeated over and over.

The central figure of the sanctuary dome in his cathedral, representing the coronation of the Blessed Virgin Mary by the Eternal Father, was painted there by his orders in memory of the cure thus obtained through her intercession.

We owe these details to Sister Stanislaus, to whom he made a full revelation of the whole occurrence a few days before his death. As he said Mass frequently at the Sacred Heart Academy this sister became well acquainted with his method of making thanksgiving after Mass, and with his habits of devotion. His close and familiar conversations with Our Lord in the Blessed Eucharist, with the Blessed Virgin, and with St. Joseph were something remarkable. She tells us that "after his usual morning Mass he would sit down and actually talk to the Blessed Virgin, telling her what she should give him, commending such and such an interest to her care."

In February, 1891, old age and over-taxed energies brought him down again and near to death's door. A circular letter of the vicar-general, sent through the diocese and to friends outside, announced what was believed to be the approach of death, and fervent prayers were sent up for him from many altars which he had helped to build, and where his face was familiar and beloved. To the surprise of all, however, he rallied so as to afford strong hope of his restoration once more to active duty. His physical condition at this time, as well as something of his warm-heartedness and the Christian tranquillity of his soul in sickness, may be seen in the following letter, dated August 31st, 1891:

"REV. DEAR FRIEND WALWORTH: I cannot tell you how grateful I feel for your most excellent and affectionate letter, through the hands of your devoted niece.

"I was brought to death's door, and received all the sacraments of Holy Church by sickness that took me to my bed on February 12th last. Since the 1st of July I have been strong enough to fast and receive Holy Communion occasionally. I went down very slowly, and very lowly, and very far; up to the present I have not been able to celebrate Mass, but am in hopes to be able to do so before many days, once in a while.

"As you well say, my working days are nearly ended as far as taking the road again. I am able to ride out every day, read a *very* little, write none.

"Your allusions to past years and our Catholic lives touch me most sensibly, but it is a matter of which I cannot write at present. Who can be more happy than we?

"With kindest and most affectionate regards and blessings for yourself and Miss Nellie,

"I am, very sincerely in Christ,

"E. P. WADHAMS, *Bishop of Ogdensburg.*"

The above letter is in the bishop's own handwriting. It begins with a certain show of firmness and good penmanship, but grows gradually more straggling, until at the close a failure of strength is very evident, and the signature is little better than a scratch.

"See what a letter I have written to you *with my own hand*," wrote St. Paul to the Galatians. Other of his inspired epistles were written in bonds and from Rome. They contain the same careful reminder that he used his own hand to write. His room in the Roman prison still remains. It was a very dark one, unless he was allowed the light of a lamp. He must have taken his scroll to the little window and written there upon the sill, on which a flush of daylight fell and still falls. It cost him something, this work of love. How affectionately he reminds his brethren of the prison which held him, and of his anxiety that they should read his heart in his own handwriting. Tears fall from my eyes when I gaze on this last letter of my old friend, and feel that it must have cost him something to trace the straggling characters with his own hand. I am not in the habit of preserving private letters, but I could not bring myself to part with this one.

Although my friend endeavored to write cheerfully, and may perhaps have entertained the prospect of resuming his active duties for a little while, yet this was not to be. There came, indeed, from time to time short periods of returning activity, as flames are seen to flicker and gleam above the dying embers of a hearth-fire; but the end soon came. He died December 5th, 1891.

The close of his last illness is thus characterized by his niece, Harriet Wadhams, wife of Dr. Stevens of New York, a most estimable lady, a Congregationalist, who was in constant attendance upon him during the last two weeks of his life. Her testimony is as follows: "It was my great privilege during this time," she says in a letter to the author, "to listen to the saintly utterances which continually fell from his lips. His end was most peaceful, as he had so long prayed that it might be."

We will not dwell upon the occurrences of that final day, nor of other days leading directly up to it, except to recall one scene remarkably characteristic, in which he signalized his departure from the world in a manner that was deliberate, solemn, and impressive.

The following account is gathered from the columns of the Ogdensburg *Courier* of December 5th, 1891:

When the symptoms of a speedy end became apparent, the bishop decided to make a final preparation for death. He was anointed and received the Holy Viaticum. His thanksgiving being ended, the bishop declared his desire to make his solemn ante-mortem declaration of faith.

There were present in the sick-chamber the Very Rev. Thomas E. Walsh, Vicar-General, and Fathers Larose, Burns, Conroy, and Murphy, priests of the diocese; his niece, Mrs. Dr. Stevens, and two members of the community of Gray Nuns, Sisters Stanislaus and Matthew.

The profession of faith according to the formula of Pius IV. was read to him in Latin. During the reading the bishop accentuated his acceptance of the church's teachings by frequently repeating, with evident satisfaction and emphasis, the words as read by Father Walsh. Now a smile of approval lit up the pallid face, now an earnest "Credo" fell from the prelate's lips. When the last words were reached a bright smile overspread the bishop's face, and he said joyously, "Deo gratias!"

This done, the dying man bethought himself of his responsibilities as a bishop. He announced that he had a last utterance to make. "You all know of my life," he said; "educated in the Protestant Episcopal belief, I left it for the One, Holy, Catholic and Apostolic Roman Church.

"It won't do to say that one church is as good as another—there is only one true church. There must be unity; there must be a head, and that is the pope. I want to insist upon unity. There may be some difference of ideas amongst us—we are of many different births—but for God's sake let there be unity amongst us. To the devoted clergy of the diocese—oh! what shall I say to them?—they have done so much for me, holding up my hands and authority—and oh!" (turning to Father Walsh) "let them hold up your hands—respect and hold up your authority! Struggle for the old faith. Be faithful in giving the Sacraments. *The priests are for the people, not the people for the priests.*" The anxious heart of the dying convert then reverted to that crowd of souls outside of the faith with which he had once been united. "If one thing has, during the past year, contributed more than another to break my health and my heart, it has been the thought that one thousand seven hundred more souls annually come into the world in this diocese than receive the sacrament of baptism. There are seven sacraments, not two only—and the saddest of it all is that even these two, once accepted, are being rejected by those who formerly accepted them." After a few more affectionate words and expressions of thanks to the clergy and religious of the diocese, and also to all the laity, he repeated once more those golden words which had been the great rule of his own life in the ministry: "THE PRIESTS ARE FOR THE PEOPLE, NOT THE PEOPLE FOR THE PRIESTS."

"I want all my priests and people to know," he concluded, "how the first bishop of Ogdensburg died." Then after a still more emphatic and closely defined declaration of his adherence to the entire faith of the church, and begging prayers to be said for him by all his people, he

TOMB OF BISHOP WADHAMS IN THE CRYPT OF THE CATHEDRAL.

requested the priests present to approach, and giving his blessing, he embraced each one in turn. All were moved to tears, and retired with sad hearts from the painful and impressive scene.

These imperfect reminiscences of the life of Bishop Wadhams are now concluded. We trust that his wish so earnestly expressed may be fulfilled, and that the Catholic people of the Adirondacks will remember how the first Bishop of Ogdensburg died. God grant, also, that all the Catholic clergy of this whole nation will treasure up the golden rule which he has bequeathed to us: "The priests are for the people, not the people for the priests."

Appendix.

The Wadhams Family in England and America.

[For the following details the author is indebted to the kindness and intelligent care of Mrs. Dr. Stevens, of New York City, daughter of William L. Wadhams.]

THE word Wadham signifies "A home by the ford." Prince, in his history entitled *Worthies of Devon*, 1701, says:

"This ancient and renowned family of Wadham had its original seat in the county of Devon and derived its name from the place of its habitation, Wadham, which is in the parish of Knowstone, near the incorporate town of South Molton. William de Wadham was a freeholder of this land in the days of King Edward I., 1272 to 1307, and both East and West Wadham descended in this name to Nicholas Wadham, founder of Wadham College, Oxford, 1609, who left them to his heirs general.

"This honorable family possessed the seat called Edge through about eight descents in a direct line, five of whom were knights, who matched with divers daughters and heirs and became allied to many great and noble houses, as Plantagenet, Worthesby, Bridges, Popham, Strangways, Tregarthian, etc., etc., as may appear from this pedigree thereof." (See *Prince's Worthies*, p. 588, folio edition, 1701.)

About the year 1499, Merrifield, an estate in Somersetshire, came into possession of Sir John Wadham by marriage, and at that time the principal seat of the family was removed to the county of Somerset. The ancient moated seat of Merrifield is in the parish of Ilton, about five miles from Ilminster to the north. St. Mary's, the parish church, was the burial-place of the family for many years, and the north aisle of the church is called the Wadham aisle because of the monuments, both mural and otherwise, there erected to the family. Nicholas Wadham and Dorothy, his wife, co-founders of Wadham College, are buried in St. Mary's Church, Ilminster. (The seal of Wadham College bears, marshalled together, the arms of Nicholas Wadham and the coat of the Petre family, his wife Dorothy having been sister of John, Lord Petre. Edgar P. Wadhams, on becoming bishop, adopted from the college seal, for his own official use, the three roses divided by a chevron which constitutes the armorial bearing of the Wadham family, with additions which have already been mentioned in the "Reminiscences.")

The first of the name to come to America was one John Wadham, who came from Somersetshire, England, and settled in Wethersfield,

Conn., in the year 1650. The line of succession from John, the first emigrant, to Bishop Wadhams is as follows:

1st. John (son of the emigrant), born at Wethersfield, July 8, 1655.
2d. Noah, of Wethersfield, born 1695.
3d. Jonathan, of   "   "   1730.
4th. Abraham, of Goshen, " 1757.
5th. Luman,   "   "   " 1782.
6th. Edgar P., of Wadhams Mills, born 1817.

It is not known who of the American family added the letter "s" to the English name of Wadham. In the early records of Connecticut it is spelled without the "s."

Nicholas, the founder of Wadham College, left no children. His father was John Wadham, Esq., of Edge, Devonshire. He had estates in both Devon and Somerset, but lived mostly in Somerset.

It is not definitely known how near the relation was between Nicholas, the founder of the college, and the John who was the first of the Wadham family to come to America. There is great probability that they were nearly related, as the same Christian names are handed down in this country as were used by the family of Nicholas in England. They were both residents of the same county.

General Luman Wadhams, father of Bishop Wadhams, was born in Goshen, Conn. He was the sixth in direct descent from John of England.

About the year 1800 he went to Charlotte, Vt., and there married the widow Lucy Prindle, born Bostwick. The first of her family to come to this country was Ebenezer Bostwick, who came from Cheshire, England, in the year 1668. About the year 1809 Luman Wadhams left Vermont and became one of the pioneer settlers of Essex County, New York, locating first in the town of Lewis, but subsequently erecting mills on the Bouquet River in the town of Westport, and laying the foundation for what has ever since been the thriving little business centre of Wadhams Mills. General Wadhams took a prominent and honorable part in the early development and the defence of Essex County. Holding the rank of general of the militia, he commanded the forces which repulsed the British when they ascended the Bouquet River in the summer of 1813, for the purpose of seizing or destroying supplies at Willsborough Falls. The fire of the militia killed or wounded nearly all that were in the rear galley on their retreat, and it floated into the lake a disabled wreck. He participated in the battle of Plattsburgh, where for three months he was on duty.

The children of General Luman Wadhams and Lucy, his wife, are as follows: Lucy Alvira, who married Dr. D. S. Wright, of Whitehall, N. Y.; Jane Ann, who married Mr. Benjamin Wells, of Upper Jay, N. Y.; William Luman, who married Emeline L. Cole, of Westport, and resided at Wadhams Mills; Abraham E., who married Sophia Southard, of Essex, N. Y., and resided at Wadhams Mills; and Edgar Prindle, the first Bishop of Ogdensburg.

THE END.

www.ingramcontent.com/pod-product-compliance
Lightning Source LLC
Chambersburg PA
CBHW020817230426
43666CB00007B/1039